A Mom's Milwaukee 2015

CALIE HERBST

Copyright © 2014 Calie Herbst

All rights reserved.

ISBN: 1501009443
ISBN-13: 9781501009440

ABOUT THE AUTHOR

Calie Herbst is a high school teacher in Milwaukee Public Schools. She started MiltownMoms.com in April of 2013. She has been featured on Fox 6's *Studia A, Real Milwaukee* and TMJ4's *Wisconsin Tonight.* Her writing has been featured on OnMilwaukee.com, mamalode.com, and InThePowderRoom.com. She has a bi-weekly parenting segment on *Wisconsin Morning News.*

She and her husband Erik are parents to Hudson (3) and Rosie (1). She currently lives with her family in the Bay View neighborhood of Milwaukee.

Painting the Milwaukee skyline at *Arte Wine and Paint Studio* in Wauwatosa.

DEDICATION

To my kids, Hudson and Rosie, who light up my life.
To my husband, Erik, who makes being married fun.
To the city of Milwaukee, for being so full of great things to do.

HOW TO USE THIS BOOK

Read it cover to cover,
flip to the section you're interested in,
or open to a random page.

Leave it on your nightstand to pick up during a rare quiet
moment, or pack it in the car to reference while you're out &
about.

Lend it to a friend
or keep it all to yourself.

ACKNOWLEDGMENTS

To the fabulous followers of MiltownMoms.com: Thank you for
your encouragement, for sharing your ideas, and for your
continued support.

To my own mom: You've shown me what it means to be a
mother. Thank you for your endless love and support.

CONTENTS

INTRODUCTION

Driving home from the hospital with my first-born son, I remember looking out of the window at an ordinary grocery store and thinking, "Nothing will ever be the same."

Now that my son was here, everything seemed new and exciting again. I saw the grocery store, and everything else, through his baby blue eyes. I couldn't wait to show him the world.

Of course, he didn't see much of the world during those first few months. He saw a lot of our living room, and the park, and happy faces of relatives. But when he turned one, and I finished my year of teaching high school full-time, I was looking forward to a whole summer of just me and my little man.

Being the organized teacher that I am, I grabbed the calendar, hopped on the internet, and began scouring local websites for fun things to do. "Oh!" I thought to myself. "A program for babies to explore nature!" I furiously jotted it down in my notebook. "Ooh," I marveled again. "A free themed story time? That sounds great." I scribbled some more. "We have to check out that nature preserve immediately," I promised myself. "And we'll definitely have to go to the free day at the museum." I couldn't believe all the interesting activities offered to families in the Milwaukee area.

But pretty soon, I felt a little overwhelmed. There was just so much stuff to do, and so many websites to visit, and I couldn't keep it all straight. Wasn't there just one place for me to go to find all of the fun kid-friendly activities happening around town each day? Surely there was.

But there really wasn't. And so MiltownMoms.com was born, and eventually, this book, too. I hope it serves as a one-stop source for you and your family to take advantage of all our city has to offer.

We all know that being a parent has its challenges. So I hope this book multiplies the fun, happy times for you and your family.

Have a great year exploring Milwaukee!

CHAPTER 1: ARTS & CRAFTS

Whether you're searching for world-class museums or a place to walk in unannounced and paint some pottery, you can find it in Milwaukee. In this chapter, explore the places in our city that allow children to tap into their inner artist. Who knows? Maybe you've got a tiny Picasso living in your midst! And if not, at least you'll have fun getting creative.

KID-FRIENDLY ART CENTERS

Latino Arts Center
1028 S 9th St.
Milwaukee, WI 53204
(414) 384-3100
http://www.latinoartsinc.org/home.htm

Latino Arts Center provides Hispanic arts programming and hands-on educational activities. Explore their gallery, the Hispanic Heritage Center and their self-guided walking tour where you can see bright, colorful murals.

Sharon Lynne Wilson Center for the Arts
19805 W. Capitol Dr.
Brookfield, WI 53045
(262) 781-9470
http://www.wilson-center.com

The Wilson Center for the Arts offers Visual Arts classes like watercolor painting and film animation for youth ages 9-16. They also feature family-friendly programming and performances throughout the year.

Walker's Point Center for the Arts
839 S. 5th St.
Milwaukee, WI 53204
(414) 672-2787
http://wpca-milwaukee.org

Walker's Point Center for the Arts is a community arts center dedicating to supporting the arts in a multicultural environment. Visit their gallery or participate in one of their kid-friendly programs or camps.

Schauer Arts & Activities Center
147 N. Rural St.
Hartford, WI 53027
(262) 670-0560
http://www.schauercenter.org

The Schauer Community School of the Arts offers year-round classes in dance, music, theater, and visual arts, for students of all ages and levels

KID-FRIENDLY ART MUSEUMS

Lynden Sculpture Garden
2145 West Brown Deer Road
Milwaukee, WI 53217
414-446-8794
http://lyndensculpturegarden.org

The Lynden Sculpture Garden offers a unique experience of art in nature through its collection of more than 50 monumental sculptures sited across 40 acres of park, lake and woodland. They offer a monthly Tuesdays in the Garden program for small children and weekly art drop-in programs for older kids.

Milwaukee Art Museum
700 Art Museum Dr.
Milwaukee, WI 53202
(414) 224-3200
http://mam.org

Kids under 12 are always admitted for free at the world-class Milwaukee Art Museum. It's also free to everyone on the first Thursday of every month. (Thanks, Target! Just one more reason why I love thee.)

Younger children will enjoy **Story Time in the Galleries** every Saturday at 10:30 a.m. Children sit beneath one of the paintings in the Gallery and enjoy a story and a craft that relates to it. They can also get creative at the **Play Date with Art**, a monthly program that includes a themed craft and singing time.

The whole family can take advantage of **ArtPacks**, which are filled with self-guided activities such as sketch-packs, scavenger hunts, and iPod Touch Tours. You can also visit **Kohl's Art Generation Open Studio,** open every Saturday and Sunday from 10:00-4:00, to create a themed art project to take home. And don't miss the high-tech, interactive **Kohl's Art Generation Lab** where you can explore what happens behind the scenes at the Museum.

Finally, the Museum hosts **Family Sundays** five times a year, where families can participate in hands-on art activities and enjoy interactive performances, family tours & visiting artists.
Be sure to check out their **Youth Studio Classes** (after school) and **Summer Art Camps** if you're child is artistically inclined (or, I suppose, if they're not

and you'd like them to be!).

Museum of Wisconsin Art (MOWA)
205 Veterans Ave.
West Bend, WI 53095
(262) 334-9638
http://www.wisconsinart.org

MOWA is the only museum in the world that is dedicated to collecting and maintaining works from Wisconsin. They offer themed Studio Saturdays every month for families to enjoy, as well as a monthly art program designed just for babies. They also offer Junior Masters studio projects designed for older kids to explore various art techniques.

PAINT-YOUR-OWN POTTERY

A Touch of Glaze
8215 Meadowbrook Rd.
Waukesha, WI 53188
(262) 524-0231
http://atouchofglaze.com/index.html

Choose from hundreds of unfinished pottery pieces to paint, and get inspiration from idea books, stamps & stencils. No reservations or experience required!

Art Trooper Studio
Audubon Court
333 W. Brown Deer Rd. - Suite T
Fox Point, WI 53217
(414) 351-1855
http://www.arttrooper.com

Art Trooper studio is where North Shore families can go to paint their own pottery, create mosaics, build with clay, venture into the world of glass fusing and more. You do not need an appointment, making it the perfect place to drop-in on a rainy day. However, they do host organized events such as birthday parties & scout group gatherings in their furnished event center.

Glaze Pottery
149 Green Bay Rd.
Thiensville, WI 53092
(262) 238-5456
http://www.glazepottery.com/index.html

Glaze Pottery features pottery, glass fusing, raw clay, and Lilly Ollo (silver clay). No reservations are required, and they also offer birthday parties, art therapy for Scout troops, church groups, schools, and corporate team building events.

Just Kiln' Time

N88W16683 Appleton Ave.
Menomonee Falls, WI 53051
(262) 255-5456
http://www.justkilntimepottery.com

Just Kiln' Time offers paint-your-own pottery, glass fusing, mosaics, metal art, canvas painting, and more. Their business was inspired by the powerful role that art can play in the livers of children with special needs and everyone else, too.

La Terraza

11520 W Bluemound Rd.
Wauwatosa, WI 53226
(414) 443-1800
http://www.potteryfun.com/parties.htm

Walk-ins are welcome at anytime at La Terraza, and all ages and experience levels will enjoy a large selection of pieces and colors. They also do birthday parties!

MOBILE ART STUDIOS

A.W.E. Truck Studio (Artists Working in Education)
http://awe-inc.org

Seeing A.W.E.'s colorful mobile art studio parked in your neighborhood is even better than the ice cream truck. These bright mini-vans are stocked with loads of art supplies and friendly artists who lead creative projects. And it's completely free! Kids can drop-in to paint, create prints, and build sculptures while learning about famous artists and basic principles of design.

Kohl's Color Wheels
http://mam.org/artgeneration/programs/kohls-color-wheels/

A mobile art experience designed for the entire family, the Kohl's Color Wheels van makes appearances at community events throughout the year, offering a variety of hands-on, engaging art projects inspired by the Museum's Collection and special exhibitions.

OTHER

Young Rembrandts Art Classes

Don & Julie Eisenhauer
262-409-1846
eisenhauers@youngrembrandts.com

Young Rembrandts offers weekly drawing classes that utilize a step by step method to assure every student is a creative success. Children discover that all complex objects can be broken down into familiar shapes; then use problem solving skills, innovation, and imagination to put them all together into eye-popping masterpieces!

CHAPTER 2: BIRTHDAY PARTIES

    This year, maybe planning a birthday party doesn't have to be stressful. Our list makes it easy to find a birthday party venue that specializes in making the day easy on you. You're bound to find something that appeals to the interests of your special kid, no matter their age.

Adventure Rock
21250 Capitol Dr.
Pewaukee, WI 53072
(262) 790-6800
http://www.adventurerock.com

Rock climbing for all ages, party area and giveaways!

Betty Brinn Children's Museum
929 E. Wisconsin Ave.
Milwaukee, WI 53202
(414) 390-KIDS (5437)
www.bbcmkids.org

Use of private party room included.

Comedy Sportz
420 S. First St.
Milwaukee, WI 53202
(414) 272-8888
www.comedysportzmilwaukee.com

Personalized party with a show specifically for Comedy Sportz Kidz.

Discovery World
500 N. Harbor Dr.
Milwaukee, WI 53202
(414) 765-8625
http://www.discoveryworld.org

Many packages available.

Engineering for Kids
Dunwood Center, Fox Point
(414) 247-1248
https://engineeringforkids.com

Hands-on engineering and robotics parties.

Just Kidding Kids Cuts
322 E. Silver Spring Dr.
Milwaukee, WI 53217
(414) 962-2524

Elaborate spa, tea and glamour parties.

Milwaukee Public Museum
800 West Wells St.
Milwaukee, WI 53233-1478
(414) 278-2714
http://www.mpm.edu

Butterfly and dinosaur themes available for all ages.

Milwaukee Recreation Department
(414) 475-8811
http://www.milwaukeerecreation.net

Carnival games, swimming and more.

Skateland
Locations in Butler, Ozaukee, Waukesha

Starz Dance Academy
S83 W18430 Saturn Dr.
Muskego, WI 53150
(262) 682-4419
http://starzdanceacademywi.com

Dance lesson and routine.

The Petite Chef
119 N. Main St.
Dousman, WI 53118
http://www.thepetitechefs.net

Cooking and baking birthday parties.

Uihlein Soccer Park
7101 W. Good Hope Rd.
Milwaukee, WI 53223
(414) 375-1153
www.mksc.org

Field time, trivia, party food and more.

Urban Ecology Center
1500 E. Park Pl.
Milwaukee, WI 53211
(414) 964-8505
http://urbanecologycenter.org

Custom "b'earthday" parties.

Wisconsin Humane Society
Milwaukee & Ozaukee campuses
http://www.wihumane.org

Tour of the shelter, play with the animals, and more.

Indoor Playgrounds & Trampoline Parks (pg. 76)
These indoor playgrounds offer high-energy, memorable birthday parties for all ages.

Bowling Alleys (pg. 124)
Find a bowling alley near you and let them take care of the details.

Paint-Your-Own-Pottery Art Studios (Pg. 14)
The five paint-your-own pottery studios around town specialize in birthday parties for your kids to get creative and do unique, personalized art projects.

Do you have something to add? Email us at
miltownmoms@gmail.com.

CHAPTER 3: SUMMER CAMPS

I grew up at YMCA Camp Minikani, where campers spend the night for a week or two, ride horses, climb the rock wall, get homesick, get over it, swim in the lake, play ridiculous games, make s'mores over crackling fires, and learn that independence can be really fun. I've included residential camps like these in this guide. But Summer Camps as a genre have blossomed into so much more, and even this s'more-loving girl has to admit that they seem pretty cool. There are day camps and workshops that appeal to every interest you can think of from zoo animals to world history. Summer is a time for your kids explore the world in a new environment, and this guide will help them do just that!

ART CAMPS

The Art of Nature
Sharon Lynne Wilson Center for the Arts
19805 W. Capitol Drive
Brookfield, WI 53045
(262) 781-9470
http://www.wilson-center.com

Explore the natural world through music, art, and dance! Teaching artists from the Wilson Center, Danceworks, The Wisconsin Conservatory of Music, and naturalists from Wehr Nature Center will help every child discover the wonderful sounds, patterns, colors, and rhythms in our own backyard. For students entering Grades 1-6.

Milwaukee Art Museum Summer Camps
700 N. Art Museum Dr.
Milwaukee, WI 53202
(414) 224-3803
http://mam.org

Build on your love of art in Museum summer camps. Be inspired by the Milwaukee Art Museum's feature exhibitions and Collection. Explore the art in the galleries during fun-filled, interactive tours, and make your own creations in hands-on projects in the Kohl's Art Generation Studio. Each class has a different focus and includes time for drawing in a personalized sketchbook. Sign up for one camp or the entire series!

The Potters' Shop Pottery Camp
335 W. Main St.
Waukesha, WI 53186
(262) 547-1920
http://www.potteryinwaukesha.com

Summer camps are taught by professional teachers in a state of the art teaching facility where children learn the basics of the craft as well as hone their skills to produce beautiful work over the course of the camp. No experience is needed and children of all ages and skill levels are invited to attend.

Summer Explore

Marquette University High School
http://www.muhs.edu/admissions/summer-explore-2014/index.aspx

Summer EXPLORE! provides learning and social opportunities for boys from all schools entering grades 5 - 9. A variety of programs are offered in Fine Arts, Technology, History, Science, German, Forensics, and Sports. Summer EXPLORE! programs are taught by current faculty, moderators and coaches with the same excellence that is the hallmark of a Marquette High education. This is an ideal time for your student to make new friends, meet teachers and coaches, and experience the Marquette High community.

Summer Youth Art Camp

Walkers Point Center for the Arts
839 South 5th St.
Milwaukee, WI 53204
(414) 672-2787
http://wpca-milwaukee.org

Walker's Point Center for the Arts organizes an extensive and affordable educational program for Milwaukee-area youth ages 6-12. Each week of Summer Art Camp is dedicated to one form of art. Sign up for one week or for all eight! Join us on an annual gallery showing of student work.

DAY CAMPS

Adventure Rock

21250 Capitol Dr.
Pewaukee, WI 53072
(262) 790-6800
http://www.adventurerock.com

Campers learn about safety systems, essential knots, proper equipment use, snacks and lots of climbing. Each themed week includes games, crafts and activities.

Adventure Summer Camp (ages 3-13)

Wehr Nature Center
9701 W. College Ave.
Franklin, WI 53132
(414) 425-8550
http://www.friendsofwehr.org

Discover the natural world with professional naturalists at Wehr Nature Center and in other Milwaukee County Parks. Offerings include fishing camps, Wildlife Adventures, and more!

Global Garden Adventures Summer Camp

Boerner Botanical Gardens
9400 Boerner Dr.
Hales Corners, WI 53130
(414) 525-5653
http://boernerbotanicalgardens.org

Themes include "All About Monarch," "Going Buggy," & "Introduction to Chinese Culture."

JCC Summer Day Camps

6255 N. Santa Monica Blvd.
Whitefish Bay, WI 53217
(414) 967-8200
https://www.jccmilwaukee.org

Camps focus on keeping campers moving, exploration, creativity, play, and Jewish values. Specialists, counselors, and artists-in-residence will expose campers to new hands on experiences.

Lynden Sculpture Gardens (ages 4-13)
2145 W. Brown Deer Rd.
Milwaukee, WI 53217
http://lyndensculpturegarden.org

Lynden's art and nature camps integrate their outdoor sculpture collection of with 40 acres of park, ponds, and woodland. Art camps feature environmental programs, visiting artists, and the opportunity to explore a wide variety of art media. Each camp concludes with an informal showing for family and friends.

Milwaukee Public Museum Summer Camps (ages 3-11)
800 West Wells St.
Milwaukee, WI 53233
http://www.mpm.edu/plan-visit/calendar/summer-camps

Day Camps at the Museum allow kids to explore the museum and engage in hands-on activities with themes such as "Animals of Africa" & "Walking with Dinosaurs" and "Native Americans: Living with the Land."

Schlitz Audubon Nature Center Summer Camps (preschool - Grade 10)
1111 E. Brown Deer Rd.
Milwaukee, WI 53217
(414) 352-2880
http://www.sanc.org

Explore 185 acres of woodlands, prairies, ponds, wetlands along the Lake Michigan shoreline, and enjoy hands-on learning with professional naturalists.

Summer Recreation Enrichment Camp
Milwaukee Recreation
5225 W. Vliet St., Room 162
Milwaukee, WI 53208
414-475-8180
http://www.milwaukeerecreation.net/srec/

Each week centered around a different theme involving sports/games, arts/crafts, outdoor education, math/reading enrichment, clubs, and field trips.

Urban Ecology Center Summer Camps (K4-grade 12)

Urban Ecology Center
1500 E. Park Pl.
Milwaukee, WI 53211
(414) 964-8505
http://urbanecologycenter.org

Explore nature with a professional environmental education staff, rock climb, do science experiments, create eco-art projects, canoe and enjoy the beaches of Lake Michigan.

Wisconsin Humane Society Summer Camps

4500 West Wisconsin Ave.
Milwaukee, WI 53208
(414) 264-6257
http://www.wihumane.org

Enjoy animal crafts, games, and furry friends at Camp Critter or explore veterinary science at Junior Veterinary Camp. Discover what it takes to become an animal doctor, learn the skills needed to work with animals, hear from professionals in the field, and practice skills in the "surgery station!"

YMCA Day Camps

Nine locations in the Greater Milwaukee Area
http://www.ymcamke.org/childcare/daycamp

Choose from "traditional" day camp, sports camps or enrichment camps. Free weekly field trips are included. Before and after care is available.

Zoological Society of Milwaukee Summer Camps (ages 2-14)

ZSM Summer Camps
10005 W. Bluemound Rd.
Milwaukee, WI 53226-4383
(414) 258-5058
http://www.zoosociety.org/Education/SummerCamps.php

The zoo offers a wide variety of themed camps featuring the animals, including "Junior Zookeepers" & "Marine Marvels."

MUSIC & DANCE CAMPS

Wisconsin Conservatory of Music
1584 N. Prospect Ave.
Milwaukee, WI 53202
(414) 276-5760
http://www.wcmusic.org

Choose from 15 themed music camps with a full-day format to fit your schedule.

DanceWorks Creative Arts Camps (ages 3-13)
1661 N. Water St.
Milwaukee, WI, 53202
(414) 277-8480
http://danceworksmke.org/classes/youth/summer-creative-arts-camps/

Camps integrate dance and visual arts, along with music, creative drama and creative writing, into one program. Each week offers a different theme to spark imagination and creativity. Camp ends with an informal performance for friends and family.

Milwaukee Youth Symphony Orchestra Camp
325 W. Walnut St.
Milwaukee, WI 53212
(414) 267-2906
http://www.myso.org/newsite/

MYSO offers music camps such as Jazz Guitar Ensemble and Calypso Steel Band Camp.

Summer Explore
Marquette University High School
http://www.muhs.edu/admissions/summer-explore-2014/index.aspx

Summer EXPLORE! provides learning and social opportunities for boys from all schools entering grades 5 - 9.

SPECIAL NEEDS

Easter Seals Summer Respite Camps
2222 S. 114th Street
West Allis, WI 53227
(414) 449-4444
http://camp.eastersealswisconsin.com

Easter Seals Southeast Wisconsin provides summer respite camp programs for children, teens and adults with or without disabilities. Our Wil-O-Way locations offer six weeks of summer fun for children and adults ages 7 and up, while our inclusive Holler Park and SPARC camps offer nine weeks of excitement for children ages 7-21.

First Stage Next Steps
325 W. Walnut St.
Milwaukee, WI 53212
(414) 267-2929
http://www.firststage.org/Our-Academy/Next-Steps/

First Stage creates a safe space for all students to be creative and be themselves without judgment or fear of failure. Next Steps classes are designed to help students with autism take their next steps as an artist and a person, allowing them the opportunity to learn social skills among their peers while participating in theatrical and musical activities.

Sensational Summer Day Camp
Milwaukee Center for Independence
Harry & Jeanette Weinberg Building
2020 W. Wells St.
Milwaukee, WI 53233
(414) 937-2020
http://www.mcfi.net/Childrens-Programs/Summer-Camp.htm

Help your child build on the progress made during the school year by participating in MCFI's Sensational Summer Day Camp. The indoor program combines social and therapeutic opportunities for children living with autism or sensory disorders. Overnight Camps

OVERNIGHT CAMPS

YMCA Camp Minikani
875 Amy Belle Rd.
Hubertus, WI 53033
(262) 251-9080
http://www.minikani.org

Located on the shores of Amy Belle Lake, 30 minutes from downtown Milwaukee, Wisconsin, YMCA Camp Minikani offers overnight camps, equestrian programs, engaging environmental education and more. But what your child really gains is confidence, new friendship and independence.

YMCA Camp Matawa
N885 Youth Camp Rd.
Campbellsport, WI 53010
(262) 626-2149
http://www.matawa.org

Located one hour north of downtown Milwaukee, YMCA Camp Matawa is nestled in the Northern Kettle Moraine State Forest.

St. John's Northwestern Military Academy Camp
1101 Genesee St.
Delafield, WI 53018
1-800-SJ-CADET (1-800-752-2338)
http://www.sjnma.org/summer-programs/summer-camp.cfm

Camp St. John's Northwestern, accredited by the American Camping Association, is an adventure camp for boys ages 11-16. The structured program combines leadership and adventure skills training with fun to promote growth in each boy's leadership, teamwork, self-confidence, and physical endurance.

SCIENCE & TECHNOLOGY CAMPS

Discovery World Summer Camps & Teen Workshops (Grades 3-8)
500 N. Harbor Dr.
Milwaukee, WI 53202
(414) 765-9966
http://www.discoveryworld.org/programs/summer-camp-and-teen-workshops/

Discovery World camps are ideal for builders, inventors, and explorers as well as those interested in technology and the environment. Guest experts and professionals in the field offer real-world experiences. Camps include Junior Fashion Designer, Robotics & Food of the Future!

Gateway Technical College
Walworth, Kenosha & Racine campuses
https://www.gtc.edu

Gateway Technical College offers hands-onactivities such as building a rocket, creating designs for hair and nails, and using a 3-D printer to design and build items.

Summer Explore
Marquette University High School
http://www.muhs.edu/admissions/summer-explore-2014/index.aspx

Summer EXPLORE! provides learning and social opportunities for boys from all schools entering grades 5 - 9. A variety of programs are offered in Fine Arts, Technology, History, Science, German, Forensics, and Sports. Summer EXPLORE! programs are taught by current faculty, moderators and coaches with the same excellence that is the hallmark of a Marquette High education. This is an ideal time for your student to make new friends, meet teachers and coaches, and experience the Marquette High community.

SPORTS CAMPS

K. Tozer Soccer Academy
(414) 368-3485
http://www.ktozersocceracademy.com

Keith Tozer, best known for being the winningest coach in indoor soccer, developed these camps to help guide young aspiring soccer players into further developing their skills, and to help teach those who are new to soccer.

Marquette University Volleyball Camps
(414) 288-6094
http://www.gomarquette.com/sports/w-volley/spec-rel/031714aaa.html

Marquette volleyball coaches and players with help campers learn new skills, while competing and having fun.

Milwaukee Baseball Academy
4200 N. Holton St. - Suite 200
Milwaukee, WI 53212
(414) 828-4777
http://milwaukeebaseballacademy.com

Milwaukee Baseball Academy offers hitting, pitching and strength camps throughout the summer.

Milwaukee Bucks Summer Basketball Camps
(414) 227-0579
http://www.nba.com/bucks/camps

Bucks camps give boys and girls (2nd grade thru age 18) the opportunity to learn the fundamentals of basketball in a fun and competitive way through league games and contests. Campers receive a Bucks Practice Jersey, Bucks Prizes throughout the week, Online Photo with Camp Team & Coach, Free Ticket Voucher to a Bucks Home Game, and special awards.

Milwaukee Kickers Soccer Camps (ages 4-14)

Uihlein Soccer Park
7101 W. Good Hope Rd.
Milwaukee, WI 53223
(414) 358-2678
http://www.mksc.org/page/show/103747-milwaukee-kickers-soccer-camps

Young campers will participate in games, activities and scrimmages designed to teach the basics of soccer. First time players are welcome! Older kids will maximize their level of skill through training techniques and games.

Milwaukee Wave Summer Camps

(414) 224-WAVE
http://www.milwaukeewave.com/youth/camps

Youth Soccer Academy Camp are led by former professional soccer players and licensed coaches. Campers will focus on fundamentals including passing, shooting, dribbling and receiving.

Kick Starters Summer Sports Camp for ages 4-8 introduces soccer skills through fun group activities, scrimmages and games. In addition to soccer, other group, sports-oriented games like dodgeball, kickball and baseball will be played. Camp coaching staff is trained and certified by the Milwaukee Kickers.

Summer Explore

Marquette University High School
http://www.muhs.edu/admissions/summer-explore-2014/index.aspx

Summer EXPLORE! provides learning and social opportunities for boys from all schools entering grades 5 - 9. A variety of programs are offered in Fine Arts, Technology, History, Science, German, Forensics, and Sports. Summer EXPLORE! programs are taught by current faculty, moderators and coaches with the same excellence that is the hallmark of a Marquette High education. This is an ideal time for your student to make new friends, meet teachers and coaches, and experience the Marquette High community.

THEATER CAMPS

First Stage Theater Academy Summer Classes
(414) 267-2970
http://www.firststage.org/Our-Academy/

First Stage Theater Academy is one of the largest theater arts education programs for young people in the country. They offer classes from beginners to advanced.

Summer Explore
Marquette University High School
http://www.muhs.edu/admissions/summer-explore-2014/index.aspx

Summer EXPLORE! offers a variety of Fine Arts Camps.

Sunset Playhouse Summer Camp
800 Elm Grove Rd.
Elm Grove, WI 53122
(262) 782-4431
http://www.sunsetplayhouse.com/education/camp.php

Sunset Playhouse offers Theater camps for ages 3-16, featuring improvisation, stage combat, musical theater and more!

Do you have something to add? Email us at
miltownmoms@gmail.com.

CHAPTER 4: COMMUNITY SERVICE
FIVE KID-FRIENDLY WAYS TO GIVE BACK

 Quality family time that doesn't involve loud television programs? A kinder, more empathetic child? Yes, please! These five community service opportunities are family-friendly, and don't take a lot of time out of your already busy schedule.

1. Paint & donate a bowl to Milwaukee Empty Bowls.

All year round, groups, troops, families and corporations come to Art Trooper to paint a bowl for Milwaukee Empty Bowls. The bowls are painted and donated to their main October fundraiser. Proceeds from the bowls go toward local hunger initiatives.

Art Trooper
Audubon Court
333 W. Brown Deer Rd.
Suite T, Fox Point, WI 53217
(414) 351-1855
http://www.arttrooper.com

2. Go toy shopping - for someone else.

Go toy shopping for somebody else who can't afford to buy them on their own. The Milwaukee Women's Center & the United Community Center are just a couple of the organizations that need your toy donations.

Milwaukee Women's Center
728 N. James Lovell St.
Milwaukee, WI 53233
(414) 449-4777
http://communityadvocates.net/women/

United Community Center
1028 S 9th St
Milwaukee, WI
(414) 384-3100
http://www.unitedcc.org/index.htm

3. Shovel snow, rake or get groceries for an older adult.

Perform outdoor seasonal tasks such as cutting grass, gardening, general yard work, raking leaves and shoveling snow for an older adult in Milwaukee County. Or help seniors and/or adults with disabilities with grocery shopping. Volunteers can either shop for or shop with a client, and arrange dates and times directly with clients. Volunteers must have own transportation. Most clients in the program are physically unable to perform these tasks, and are not able to pay a service. Volunteers are matched with clients who live as close to them as possible. They might be right on the same block! The first requirement is to fill out a volunteer application. Volunteers will need to provide their own transportation and must be physically able to do the work.

Interfaith Older Adult Programs
600 W. Virginia Avenue - Suite 300
Milwaukee, WI 53204
(414) 291-7500
http://home.interfaithmilw.org

4. Organize a supply drive

If you're feeling a little more ambitious, help your child organize a supply drive in your neighborhood, Scout troop, or school for used clothing, baby equipment, books and toys. The items will then be distributed to families in need at the Northwest Trading Post at Holy Cross Lutheran Church in Menomonee Falls.

Northwest Trading Post
Holy Cross Lutheran Church
W156n8131 Pilgrim Rd.
Menomonee Falls, WI 53051
(262) 251-2740
http://www.holycrosslutheran.org

5. Organize a litter clean-up team with Keep Greater Milwaukee Beautiful.

Gather a group to clean up trash and beautify your space, help sort, count and take inventory of shoes that will be recycled into new playgrounds, or help tend to raised garden beds and beautify outdoor spaces.

Keep Greater Milwaukee Beautiful
1313 W. Mt Vernon Ave.
Milwaukee, WI 53233
(414) 272-5462
http://www.kgmb.org

Do you have something to add? Email us at
miltownmoms@gmail.com.

CHAPTER 5: COOKING CLASSES

Who knew there were so many great opportunities in Milwaukee for kids to learn to cook? From informal Mexican cooking classes to ongoing culinary arts classes, your kid will be cooking dinner for your whole family in no time. And that, of course, means less work for you. Bon appetit!

Braise Restaurant & Culinary School
1101 S. 2nd St.
Milwaukee, WI 53204
(414) 212-8843

Braise offers occassional kids cooking classes such as "Oodles of Noodles" for children ages 9 and up. They also hold classes for adults.

Chiquito's Cooking Classes (Free!)
Senor Tomas (Hartland) and Antigua Real (Mukwonago)
http://anaandzelli.com

Learn how to cook delicious Mexican dishes and start learning a little Spanish at the same time! These classes are free.

Superior Equipment & Supply Cooking Classes
4550 South Brust Ave.
Milwaukee, WI 53235
1-800-960-4300
https://www.superiorequipmentsupplies.com

Young chefs will be introduced to cooking vocabulary & techniques, tools and utensils, basics of etiquette, nutrition, safety, math and new foods.

The Petite Chef
119 N. Main St.
Dousman, WI 53118
(262) 431-4026
http://www.thepetitechefs.net

The Petite Chef offers cooking classes and parties for groups of all ages. In a commercial kitchen, kids learn basic cooking techniques, knife skills, and food safety while being supervised by a personal chef.

The Secret Oven
Fox Point
http://www.thesecretoven.com

In small, hands-on classes, kids learn basic skills needed to make nutritious foods. The Secret Oven uses all natural, organic, and local ingredients whenever possible and only natural food colorings derived from plants and vegetables.

William Sonoma Junior Chef's Cooking Classes
Mayfair Mall location
http://www.mayfairmall.com/events

Junior Chef's Cooking Classes with themes such as smoothie-making and homemade ice cream. Check Mayfair Mall's calendar of events.

CHAPTER 6: DANCE LESSONS

Whether your child wants to be a professional ballerina, a hip-hop dancer in music videos, or if you're just looking for a fun way to get them exercising, explore the many options Milwaukee has to offer.

Academy of Classical Ballet
3211 S. Lake Dr.
St. Francis, WI 53235
(414) 243-5171
http://www.milwaukeekidsdance.com

Academy of Classical Ballet is a nationally recognized ballet school. Check out their popular Mommy & Me class for 16 mo.-3 yr. olds.

Academy of Dance Arts
9036 N. 51st St.
Brown Deer, WI 53223
(414) 354-8020
http://adaofwisc.com

Academy of Dance Arts offers classes in Ballet, Jazz, Tap, Hip-Hop, Pointe, Modern, and Irish. It is a performance based school and provides opportunities for the dancers to perform at a variety of different venues. Students at ADA have performed at Milwaukee Wave Games, Summerfest, Festal Italiana, Lakefront Festival of the Arts, July 4th Celebrations, State Fair, Nursing Homes, Disney World, and the Macy's Thanksgiving Day Parade.

Bella Via Dance Studio
1220 W. Ranchito Ln. - Unit C
Mequon, WI 53092
(262) 236-9298
http://www.bellaviadancestudio.com

Bella Via Dance Studio offers dance classes in a variety of genres by professional educators. Children will enhance their physical coordination and agility, as well as their creativity and academic aptitude.

Dancercise Kids Studio Saturdays
www.creativecaterpillarkids.com

Dancercise Kids incorporates fitness, muscle education, various styles of dance (ballet, jazz, tap), creative movements, gymnastics and American Sign Language. The program follows a monthly curriculum of weekly 30 minute classes. The units focus on healthy habits, occupations, manners, musical instruments and more.

Danceworks

1661 N. Water St.
Milwaukee, WI 53202
(414) 277-8480
http://danceworksmke.org

Danceworks offers 90 different classes each week at the downtown Water
Street studio, with additional satellite classes held at the Harry & Rose Samson
Family Jewish Community Center (JCC) in Whitefish Bay and the Milwaukee
Youth Arts Center (MYAC) downtown.

Milwaukee Ballet School & Academy

8665 N. Port Washington Rd.
Fox Point, WI 53217
(414) 228-8128
http://www.milwaukeeballetschool.org

Starz Dance Academy

S83 W18430 Saturn Dr.
Muskego, WI 53150
(262) 682-4419
http://starzdanceacademywi.com

Starz Dance Academy offers studio classes, a competitive pom program, dance
fitness classes, birthday parties & more!

Do you have something to add? Email us at
miltownmoms@gmail.com.

CHAPTER 7: DAY TRIPS

(Bookworm Gardens in Sheboygan offers two acres of literature-themed gardens and exhibits.)

Sometimes you just have to get out of **Dodge**, as they say. Or, in this case, get out of Milwaukee. In this chapter, we offer 21 ideas for day trips within a few hours of Milwaukee.

Above & Beyond Children's Museum

902 N. 8th St.
Sheboygan, WI 53081
http://abkids.org

Almost 10,000 square feet of exhibit space on three floors and a mezzanine offer a vast interactive environment where families can discover and learn together.

America's Action Territory Family Fun Park

12345 75th St.
Kenosha, WI 53142
(262) 857-7000
http://www.actionterritory.com

A family fun park featuring go-karts, miniature golf, batting cages, paint ball, and arcade.

Animal Gardens Theme Park

5065 Hwy. 50
Delavan, Wisconsin, 53115
http://www.animalgardens.com

Animal Gardens Theme Park is a 40-acre venue which serves as home to The Dancing Horses Theater and Echo the talking and singing parrot, most noted for his recent appearances on America's Got Talent. You'll find 16 species of exotic animals and over 60 hay-eating animals. Visit the interactive Baby Animal Barn where you can pet, hold and feed exotic and farm animal babies. Then, roam or ride the manicured trails. Visit the deer park where you can hand-feed the deer. Venture to the Indian Village, the interactive petting zoo, and the pond, where you can enjoy a boat ride and paddle with the swans.

Open between May 1 and Oct. 31.

Bay Beach Amusement Park

1313 Bay Beach Rd.
Green Bay, WI
(920) 448-3365
http://greenbaywi.gov/baybeach/

Bay Beach is a municipal amusement park in Green Bay, Wisconsin. Situated near the mouth of the Fox River, on the east bank as it flows into Green Bay, the park contains a ferris wheel, bumper cars and boats, a giant slide, concessions, a roller coaster & more!

Bay Beach Wildlife Sanctuary
1660 East Shore Dr.
Green Bay, WI 54302
(920) 391-3671
http://www.baybeachwildlife.com

The Bay Beach Wildlife Sanctuary is a beautiful 700 acre urban wildlife refuge featuring live animal exhibits, educational displays, miles of hiking/skiing trails and various wildlife viewing opportunities. It is the largest park in the Green Bay Park system and home to the second largest wildlife rehabilitation program in Wisconsin, caring for more than 4,500 orphaned and injured animals annually.

Bookworm Gardens
1415 Campus Dr.
Sheboygan, WI 53081
(920) 287-7895
http://www.bookwormgardens.org

Bookworm Gardens is a vibrant, playful children's garden based completely on children's literature. The two acre garden offers the young and young at heart the opportunity for free, unstructured play in a beautiful and secure environment. Entrance to the garden is free. You can explore outdoor classrooms, a small amphitheater, a greenhouse, an outdoor creation station, and plenty of nooks and crannies for reading.

Cave of the Mounds
2975 Cave of the Mounds Rd.
Blue Mounds, Wisconsin 53517-0148
(608) 437-3038
http://www.caveofthemounds.com

Cave of the Mounds National Natural Landmark is celebrating 75 years as the premier cave in the upper Midwest and the jewel box of America's major show caves. Guided tours of this geologic wonder follow paved, lighted walkways departing regularly everyday of the year.

Tours pass colorful crystal formations on paved lighted walkways. You can also visit the gemstone mine, butterfly gardens, and hiking and biking trails, Birthday Party Packages, Camps, School and Scout Programs are also available. It is located 20 minutes west of Madison, off U.S. Highways 18/151.

Cedarburg Historic District
http://www.cedarburg.org

Located just 22 miles north of Milwaukee, historic Cedarburg offers fun for the whole family. Browse through the shops in the Cedar Creek Settlement, check out the General Store Museum and enjoy a walk over the last covered bridge in Wisconsin in Covered Bridge Park.

Dan Patch Stables
Lake Geneva
(262) 215-5303
http://www.danpatchstables.com

Dan Patch Stables offers a free petting farm, pony rides and trail rides. Trail rides are available seven days a week by reservation.

Dinosaur Discovery Museum
5608 Tenth Ave.
Kenosha, Wisconsin
(262) 653-4450
http://www.kenosha.org/wp-dinosaur/

The main gallery of the Dinosaur Discovery Museum is a primer on dinosaurs – what they were, how we know they existed, what they looked like, how they behaved, how and why they were alike and different, and what happened to them.

The dinosaur skeletons in the main gallery are casts of actual dinosaur fossil bones. Each dinosaur is labeled with information about the species. Panels on the gallery wall answer the most-asked questions about dinosaurs. You can listen to the environmental and animal sounds in the exhibit gallery. Step back into the Mesozoic era with outdoors sounds in different terrains and weather conditions during the Age of Dinosaurs.

Ella's Deli & Ice Cream Parlor
2902 East Washington Ave.
Madison, WI 53704
(608) 241-5291
http://www.ellasdeli.com

Youngsters will be mesmerized by the animated displays that fill the restaurant from floor to ceiling, the glass top tables containing model trains chugging though tiny towns, and marble maze races to test their dexterity. The special two-page kids' menu offers classic choices of cheeseburgers and hot dogs, matzo ball soup, and the Humpty Dumpty sundae. In the spring, summer, and fall, you can ride on the 1927 fully restored Parker Carousel.

Henry Vilas Zoo (Free!)
702 South Randall Ave.
Madison, WI 53715-1665
(608) 266-4732
http://www.vilaszoo.org

Henry Vilas Zoo is a 28-acre public zoo in Madison, Wisconsin. Owned by the city of Madison, the zoo charges no admission or parking fees. It receives over 750,000 visitors annually. The zoo houses an African lion, chimpanzees, a red panda and more!

Holy Hill
1525 Carmel Rd.
Hubertus, WI 53033
(262) 628-1838
https://www.holyhill.com

Visit Holy Hill's 435 acres of nature and climb their lookout tower to see a spectacular view.

House on the Rock
5754 State Rd. 23
Spring Green, WI 53588
(608) 935-3639
http://www.thehouseontherock.com

Marvel at the House itself, an engineering and artistic masterpiece, and check out the eclectic, exotic and whimsical collections and displays. On your self-guided tour you will explore The Infinity Room, extending an unsupported length of 218 feet and soaring 156 above the valley floor, The World's Largest Carousel featuring 269 handcrafted animals, 20,000 lights and 182 chandeliers, an enormous sea creature longer than the Statue of Liberty is tall, and a Japanese Garden including 14 foot quadruple waterfalls cascading into a garden pond.

Kenosha Public Museum
5500 1st Ave.
Kenosha, WI 53140
(262) 653-4140
http://www.kenosha.org/wp-museum/

The Kenosha Public Museum is a natural sciences and fine and decorative arts museum that is home to exhibits featuring mammoths, world cultures, Native Americans, zoology, geology, fossils, and fine and decorative arts. The Field Station section offers hands-on activities especially for kids. Take a closer look at insects, fossils, and shells and identify the neighborhood birds.

Legoland Discovery Center
Streets of Woodfield
601 N. Martingale Rd.
Schaumburg, IL 60173
http://www.legolanddiscoverycenter.com/chicago/

Visit LEGOLAND® Discovery Center Chicago at Streets of Woodfield, Schaumburg, and jump into the World's biggest box of LEGO® bricks. Inside the Center you can learn tips from a Master Model Builder, join your favorite LEGO characters in a 4D cinema, pedal on a Technicycle Ride and build LEGO creations.

Little Amerricka Amusement Park
700 E. Main St.
Marshall, WI 53559
http://www.littleamerricka.com

Little Amerricka features twenty-six rides and attractions including a classic 1950's Wooden Roller Coaster The Meteor and other restored rides from classic amusement parks of a bygone era.

Possibility Playground (Free!)
Upper Lake Park
Port Washington, WI 53074
http://possibilityplayground.org

Possibility Playground was built with children of all types of physical abilities in mind. It overlooks Lake Michigan and offers a variety of unique sensory stations for kids to explore.

Six Flags Great America
1 Great America Pkwy.
Gurnee, IL 60031
(847) 249-1776
https://www.sixflags.com/greatamerica

Six Flags Great America is a massive amusement park featuring over 100 rides and attractions.

West Bend
http://visitwestbend.com

West Bend is located in the hills of the Kettle Moraine and offers four museums, including the new Museum of Wisconsin Art. Explore nature trails, parks, a historic downtown and a variety of community events. West Bend is known as the Geocaching Capital of the Midwest™ and is a favorite destination for treasure hunters from around the region.

See also: State Parks within an hour of Milwaukee (pg. 107)

Do you have something to add? Email us at
miltownmoms@gmail.com.

CHAPTER 8: FAMILY-FRIENDLY RESTAURANTS

(Enjoy a nutritious smoothie at Refuge Smoothie, where kids get $2.00 smoothies on weekends)

We've all been there - a screaming toddler, a crying baby, fighting siblings, and irritated restaurant patrons scowling at you. Stick to the restaurants on this list so you won't have to feel quite so terrible if things get out of control. Some of the restaurants have price specials, game rooms, or separate family dining rooms for kids and families.

Blaze Pizza

17530 W. Blue Mound Rd.
Brookfield, WI 53045
(262) 754-0999
http://www.blazepizza.com

The pizza is fresh, nutritious and completely customizable. The space is modern, clean and welcoming. The service is quick and friendly.

Classic Slice

2797 S. Kinnickinnic Ave.
Milwaukee, WI 53207
(414) 238-2406
http://theclassicslice.com

Huge slices of pizza that could feed your whole family! There are always plenty of families in this casual pizzeria, so you won't get the evil eye when your toddler throws a fork across the room.

The Chancery

4624 S. 27th St., Milwaukee
7615 W. State St., Wauwatosa
11046 N. Port Washington Rd., Mequon
http://www.thechancery.com

Free popcorn while you wait, an extensive kids menu, live music and more. Tuesday is Kid's Day: kids pay their height for each kid's meal, only a penny per inch. At the Milwaukee location, dress as your favorite superhero and receive a free ice cream sundae!

Fazoli's

10833 W. Greenfield Ave.	3800 S. Moorland Rd.	6930 75th S.t
West Allis, WI 53214	New Berlin, WI 53151	Kenosha, WI 53142

http://www.fazolis.com

Fazoli's offers fresh-made pastas, oven-baked pastas, and more. Tuesday night is kids night, when you can get two kids' meals at 99 cents each with one adult entree. Participate in their kids' program, Spaghetti Smarts, featuring coloring sheets and activities.

Fish Fry in the Parks
Brown Deer Golf Clubhouse
Whitnall Park Golf Clubhouse
Grant Park Golf Clubhouse
http://milwaukeecountygolfcourses.com/golf/proto/
milwaukeecountygolfcourses2/shared_fishfry/shared_fishfry.htm

Memorial Day through Labor Day, enjoy your Friday night fish fry in the
beautiful surroundings of the Milwaukee County Parks.

Highland House
12741 N. Port Washington Rd.
Mequon, WI 53092
(262) 243-5844
http://highlandhouse.ws/site/

Just one mile north of North Shore Marcus Theaters, this Carribean-style
restaurant offers plenty of options for all ages. There is even a video game
room for your antsy ones.

Hubbard Park Lodge
3565 N. Morris Blvd.
Milwaukee, WI 53211
(414) 332-4207
http://www.hubbardlodge.com

Located in picturesque Hubbard Park on the Milwaukee River, their Sunday
Lumberjack Brunch includes warm, fried donuts, family-style plates of
pancakes, eggs, hashbrowns and breakfast sausage and bacon, an omelette bar
and a selection of fresh fruits, cereals and juices. The log cabin feel is cozy and
inviting for your whole family. All this for $11.95 per adult and $4.95 per child
12 & under. Children under two eat free. Park in the parking lot at the
intersection of North Morris Blvd. and E. Menlo Blvd. Access the park and
lodge through a pedestrian tunnel running under the Oak Leaf Trail. Your kids
will love this short nature walk, and you'll need to burn off some extra calories
on the way home.

Kopp's Frozen Custard

5373 N. Port Washington Rd., Glendale, WI
7631 W. Layton Ave., Greenfield, WI
18880 W. Blue Mound Rd., Brookfield, WI
http://www.kopps.com

An old favorite with classic custard, fried foods, and family-friendly outdoor seating.

Maxie's Southern Comfort

6732 W. Fairview Ave.
Milwaukee, WI 53213
(414) 292-3969
http://maxies.com/milwaukee/

Maxie's southern inspiration includes the "Low Country" cooking of the Carolinas, Creole and Cajun cooking of Louisiana, traditional slow-smoked southern barbeque, and southern comfort cooking of all kinds. They feature a raw bar serving fresh oysters, clams and shrimp flown in 5 days a week from the some of the best fish purveyors on the east coast. Sunday is Family Night when kids 12 and under eat for $1.00.

Melthouse Bistro

1857 E. Kenilworth Place
Milwaukee, WI 53202
(414) 271-MELT (6358)
http://www.melthousebistro.com

Melthouse Bistro features hand-crafted, gourmet grilled cheese sandwiches made with Wisconsin cheese and fresh-baked artisan breads. Kids eat free every Sunday!

Mia Famiglia

10049 W. Forest Home Ave.
Hales Corners, WI, USA
(414) 425-0507
http://www.miafamigliarestaurant.com

Mia Famiglia offers home-made breads, soups, handmade pastas and deserts, herb-infused oils and Italian entrées. All their ingredients are local and they are celiac certified, so their whole menu can be made gluten-free. Their tiramisu is made from scratch. Relax on their patio or in their casual dining area. Tuesday-Thursday:, one kid 12 & under gets a free kid's meal per adult full size entree purchase!

Mineshaft
22 N. Main St.
Hartford, WI 53027
(262) 673-5416
http://www.mineshaftrestaurant.com

The Mineshaft offers an extensive "Just for Kids" menu and a huge gameroom!

Nines American Bistro
12400 N. Ville Du Parc Dr.
Mequon, WI 53092
(262) 518-0129
http://www.ninesmequon.com

Nines American Bistro offers a more formal dining room or a casual sports bar atmosphere with 13 HD TVs. The Playdium Game room features 4000 square feet of interactive games for kids. They even offer programming of kids on the weekends so you can enjoy a date night.

North Star American Bistro
4518 N. Oakland Ave. (Shorewood)
19115 W. Capitol Dr. (Brookfield)
http://northstarbistro.com

Enjoy traditional American favorites, along with more sophisticated fare, at this upscale but casual eatery. Both locations have a separate family dining room! At the Shorewood location, the family section has toys, a chalkboard and ample play space. There is a full children's menu, and kids eat free on Sundays.

Organ Piper Pizza
4353 S. 108th St.
Greenfield, WI 53228
(414) 529-1177
http://www.organpiperpizza.com

This Milwaukee landmark, opened in 1976, boasts highly rated thin crust pizza and the country's finest organists to entertain you.

Original Pancake House
2621 N. Downer Ave
Milwaukee, WI 53211
(414) 431-5055
http://www.originalpancakehouse.com

Expect a bit of a wait, fresh orange juice, especially delicious pancakes, and omelets the size of your head! There are always plenty of families here and the comfortable large booths are perfect for an outing with the kids.

Refuge Smoothies
Downtown: 763 N. Plankinton Ave.
East Side: 2328 N. Farwell Ave.
Bay View: 422 E. Lincoln Ave.
(414) 278 6015
http://refugesmoothies.com

On Saturdays and Sundays, kids receive $2.00 smoothies!

(WORTH A DAY TRIP)

Ella's Deli & Ice Cream Parlor
2902 East Washington Ave., Madison, WI 53704
(608) 241-5291
info@ellasdeli.com

Youngsters will be mesmerized by the animated displays that fill the restaurant from floor to ceiling, the glass top tables containing model trains chugging though tiny towns, and marble maze races to test their dexterity. The special two-page kids' menu offers classic choices of cheeseburgers and hot dogs, matzo ball soup, and the Humpty Dumpty sundae. In the spring, summer, and fall, you can ride on the 1927 fully restored Parker Carousel.

Do you have something to add? Email us at
miltownmoms@gmail.com.

CHAPTER 9: FARMER'S MARKETS

Enjoying local Wisconsin goods and produce is one of the many perks of living here. You can find these products at one of the nearby farmer's markets throughout the entire year. Many of the markets offer live music, kids' activities and free samples. It's the perfect way to spend quality time as a family and while away a Summer (or Winter) day.

SUMMER FARMER'S MARKETS

Delafield Farmer's Market
Saturdays in May through October
8:00 - 1:00, rain or shine
Historic downtown Delafield, next to the Fish Hatchery Building
http://www.delafieldfarmersmarket.com

Delafield Farmer's Market is an open-air, producer-only, Public Market and admission is always free. All vendors are local within a 50 mile radius and offer a variety of fruits & vegetables along with specialty food and bakery items, honey, maple syrup, eggs, meat, poultry, fish. Artisan wares and on-site food are for sale, as well.

Cedarburg Farmer's Market
Fridays in June through October
9:00-2:00
Mill & Washington
http://www.cedarburg.org

Cedarburg Farmer's Market offers a wide variety of fresh farm produce, organic foods, flowers, herbs and perennials, fresh coffee, bakery and artisan crafts.

East Town Market
Saturdays June through early October
9:00-1:00
Cathedral Square Park
http://www.easttown.com/events/east-town-market

Enjoy fresh produce, locally made crafts, prepared foods, live entertainment and great activities. Over 100 Wisconsin farmers, craftsmen, bakers and chefs offer seasonal, fresh and unique items. Everything is made or grown locally. Activities include yoga sponsored by the WAC starting at 9am, live music, dance lessons from Danceworks and more!

East Side Green Market
Saturdays June-October
10:00-2:00
Beans and Barley parking lot
1901 E North Ave.
Milwaukee, WI 53202
(414) 502-9489
http://www.theeastside.org/categories/10-green-market

The East Side Green Market features locally grown produce, local artists, designers & craftspeople, sustainable living/growing demonstrations, local food & drinks and local entertainment!

Garden District Farmer's Market
Saturdays June-October
1:00-5:00
6th Street and Howard Ave.
http://www.gardendistrictfarmersmarket.com

Located directly across from the Art Deco Town of Lake Water Tower at 6th and Howard, the Garden District Farmers' Market is a jewel along Milwaukee's Green Corridor running along 6th Street from Howard to College Avenues on Milwaukee's south side.

Greenfield Farmer's Market
Sundays June-October
10:00-2:00
Konkel Park
5151 W. Layton Ave.
http://greenfieldfarmersmarket.com

Milwaukee Public Market Outdoor Urban Market
Early June-October
400 N. Water Street
Milwaukee, WI 53202
(414) 336-1111
http://www.milwaukeepublicmarket.org/outdoor-urban-market.html

Located in Milwaukee's charming and unique Third Ward, the Urban Market offers fresh seasonal produce and regional artists.

New Berlin Farmer's Market
Saturdays May-October
8:00-12:00
New Berlin Municipal Building
16300 W. National Ave.
http://www.newberlinchamber.org/pages/FarmersMarket/

The New Berlin Farmers Market offers a wide variety of fresh, locally grown goods including flowers, fresh vegetables, homemade bakery, salsa, and more.

Oconomowoc Summer Farmer's Market
Saturdays May-October
7:00-12:00
South Municipal Parking Lot behind 175 E Wisconsin Ave.
http://www.oconomowoc.org/events/summer-farmers-market/

South Shore Farmer's Market
Saturdays mid-June-mid-October
8:00-12:00
South Shore Park
http://southshorefarmersmarket.com

The South Shore Farmers' Market is located in beautiful Bay View directly across from Lake Michigan.

Tosa Farmer's Market
Saturdays starting in June
8:00-12:00
Downtown Tosa
http://tosafarmersmarket.com

The Tosa Farmers Market offers an array of produce, seedlings, cut flowers, prepared food from local vendors, good coffee and the happy faces of friends and neighbors.

Walker Square Farmer's Market
Sundays, Tuesdays & Thursdays June through October
8:00 a.m.-5:00 p.m.
Walker Square Park
http://walkersquare.org

Walker Square Park offers convenient parking, public restrooms, a newly designed and constructed playground, a wading pool, bicycle racks, plenty of green space and abundant shade!

Waukesha Farmer's Market
Saturdays May-October
8:00-12:00
Historic Downtown Waukesha in Riverfront Plaza
http://www.waukeshafarmersmarket.com

The Waukesha Farmers' Market is an open air, producer-only market that features vendors who sell what they grow, harvest, raise, and produce. All produce and products available at the market have either been grown, processed, or crafted by the participating vendors.

West Allis Farmer's Market
May - November
Tuesday, Thursday
12:00 pm - 6:00 pm
Saturday
1:00 pm - 6:00 pm
6501 W. National Ave.
http://www.westalliswi.gov/?nid=201

The West Allis Farmer's Markets opens later in the day to allow the farmers to bring only the freshest produce, picked that morning, to the market. Farmers may leave earlier if all produce has been sold. A wide range of produce arrives at the market throughout the year. The early season brings bedding plants, radishes, asparagus, and rhubarb. Strawberries and raspberries arrive in June as well as zucchini, squash, peas, snap beans. Corn arrives about a week after July 4 along with many other squashes and herb plants. The late season brings fresh apples and cider. Chickens and fresh eggs are always available.

West Town Farmer's Market

Wednesdays June–October
10:00-3:00
Zeidler Union Square
http://www.westown.org/neighborhood-events/westown-farmers-market

The Westown Farmers' Market features more than 60 vendors selling Wisconsin-grown produce and flowers, delicious prepared food items, handcrafted art and jewelry, lunch from area restaurants, chef demonstrations, and live music in the park's gazebo.

WINTER FARMER'S MARKETS

Milwaukee County Winter Farmer's Market
Saturdays throughout the Winter
9:00-1:00
Mitchell Park Domes
524 S. Layton Blvd
Milwaukee, WI 53204
http://www.mcwfm.org

Get free admission to the Domes and explore the Milwaukee County Winter
Farmer's Market. Enjoy story time and the toy train exhibit in the Show Dome,
and check out all the local vendors selling produce, meats. bakery and more.

St. Ann's Indoor Farmer's Market
Saturdays throughout the Winter
St. Ann's Center for Intergenerational Care
2801 E. Morgan Ave.
Milwaukee, WI 53207
http://www.stanncenter.org/farmersmarket

Saturdays; Featuring fresh seasonal, natural & organic
produce, preserves ,canned goods, homemade items, jams &
jellies, soups, soaps, lotions & makeup, and jewelry

CHAPTER 10: FALL FUN
APPLE PICKING, PUMPKIN PATCHES
& SPECIAL EVENTS

Nothing beats a crisp Fall morning in southeastern Wisconsin. You can pick juicy apples at local farms, savor homemade cider donuts, and choose the perfect pumpkin for the front porch. Explore our ideas to create your perfect Fall weekend.

APPLE ORCHARDS

Apple Holler
5006 S. Sylvania Ave.
Sturtevant, WI 53177
(262) 884-7100
appleholler.com

At Apple Holler, you can pick many varieties of apples. Your kids can also explore the Farm Park, including a corn maze, an animal feeding area, pony rides, tractor tours, and a giant slide. Pumpkins are available in October, as well.

Awe's Apple Orchard
8081 S. 100th St.
Franklin, WI 53132
(414) 425-1426
https://plus.google.com/113384295016746051068/about?gl=us&hl=en

To the south of the city, nestled on a little pond along Highway 100 in the city of Franklin, you'll spot **Awe's Apple Orchard**. Even the gravel path leading to the main orchard area is lined with beautiful apple trees to entice you. You'll drive past the quaint pond, enormous old trees, and fall-themed scarecrows. Adjacent to the parking lot, you'll spot the store and the white tent where you purchase your apple picking bags.

Awe's Orchard is not huge, but it's smaller size contributes to its charm. When I visited, we picked McIntosh, Golden Delicious and Honeycrisp apples, and we got excited for Halloween seeing their sizable pumpkin patch. But perhaps the best part of our visit to Awe's was trying their homemade cider donuts. They are fried and crispy on the outside, and perfectly soft on the inside. It's the perfect way to reward yourself for all that rigorous apple picking you did.

Visit the apple house for fresh picked apples, Apple Cider, Apple Cider Donuts, Apple Crisp Mix, Jam's, Jellies, and gifts.

Barthel Fruit Farm

12246 N. Farmdale Rd.
Mequon, WI 53097
(262) 242-2737
http://www.barthelfruitfarm.com/

Far from strip malls and city life, Barthel Fruit Farm is expansive, and their apple-picking process is a well-oiled machine. You'll veer right to visit the store located inside the farm, and you'll go left to pick your own.

The drive-by attendant will provide you with all the information you need, as well as the bags for picking. Pay on the way out at their drive-through register. If you want to pick up a caramel apple to end the experience, you can park off to the right before you exit and visit the store.

The highlight of our trip to Barthel's was their magical plum orchard. You'll feel as though you're walking through a fairy tale as you roam through rows of plum trees bursting with blue and purple ripened plums ready for the picking.

Barthel Fruit Farm offers pumpkins later in the season, too.

Basse's Country Delight

S70W16050 Janesville Rd.
Muskego, WI 53150, Waukesha L, Muskego, WI 53150
(414) 422-0315
http://www.bassescountrydelight.com/

Enjoy sweet corn, apples, pumpkins, a petting zoo, and Pumpkin Fest.

Elegant Farmer

1545 Main St.
Mukwonago, WI 53149
(262) 363-6770
http://www.elegantfarmer.com

Check out their Harvest Festival on weekends in September and October. You can pick a variety of apples and pumpkins, too. Enjoy hayrides, train rides, a corn maze, and of course, their cider donuts.

Nieman Orchards
9932 Pioneer Rd.
Cedarburg, WI 53012
(262) 377-4284
http://www.niemanorchards.com
MiltownMoms.com pick!

The Old Red Barn is rustic and filled with Neiman Orchards' own products, such as their delicious homemade cider. Inside the Barn, you purchase your picking bags. They look small, but they are deceptive. You can fit more apples than you can eat inside even the smallest bag. But if you're an apple enthusiast or baker, it may be fun to use one of their vintage wooden baskets to collect your fruit.

Behind the farm, an old fashioned wagon is waiting for you and your family to climb aboard. They'll take you on a short ride out to the orchard, sans seat belts, doors, or anything else that might prevent a lawsuit. It feels old-fashioned and authentic.

At 4 p.m. on the day we visited, the sun was low and it lit up the fields. My son and nephew were entranced with the bright red apples they saw dangling off the trees on the way to our picking destination. We were given no rules and no limits. We were just told to "pick what looks good." We wandered around the rows and rows of apple trees, seeing nothing else in any direction. When we were finished, the wagon took us back to the barn.

Neiman Orchards also offers pick-your-own pumpkins in September and October.

Peck & Bushel Fruit Company (Organic)
5472 County Road Q, Colgate, WI 53017
(414) 418-0336
http://peckandbushel.com
MiltownMoms.com pick!

It may be a bit of a drive from Milwaukee, but a visit to Wisconsin's only organic apple orchard is worth it. You will never eat a honey crisp apple that tastes better than the ones they grow here. Check their website for pick-your-own dates and times.

PUMPKIN PATCHES

Many of the apple orchards listed in the previous section offer pumpkin picking, as well. Here are additional places for pumpkin picking and Fall fun:

Bear Den Zoo and Petting Farm

6831 Big Bend Rd.
Waterford, WI 53185
(262) 895-6430
http://www.beardenzoo.com

Pick your own pumpkins or buy already picked pumpkins and produce. Also enjoy tractor-pulled hay rides, pony rides, a petting zoo, farm animals and the haunted woods!

Godsell Farm

S105w15585 Loomis Dr.
Muskego, WI 53150
(414) 425-2937
http://www.godsellfarm.com

Pick your own pumpkins or choose from already picked pumpkins. Feed the animals and enjoy a hayride.

Homestead Animal Farm

W320 N9127 Highway 83
Hartland, WI 53029
(262) 966-3840
http://www.homesteadanimalfarm.com

Buy already picked pumpkins, gourds, squash, indian corn and more. Have fun in the corn maze, enjoy a tractor-pulled hay rides, and meet the farm animals.

Jim's Pumpkin Farm
N124W17781 Lovers Ln.
Germantown, WI 53022
262) 251-0463
http://www.jimspumpkinfarm.com

Pick your own pumpkins or choose from already picked pumpkins, indian corn, gourds and more. Also hop on a hayride or get lost in the corn maze.

Land of the Giants Pumpkin Farm
11823 HWY 11
Sturtevant, WI 53177
(262) 886-6690
http://www.giantpumpkinfarm.com

See giant pumpkins, choose from an assortment of picked pumpkins, gourds and squash, and enjoy a corn maze, tractor-pulled hay rides, wagon rides, a petting zoo and more.

Lindners Pumpkin Farm and Corn Maze
19075 W. Cleveland Ave.
New Berlin, WI 53146
(262) 549-5364
http://www.lindnerspumpkinfarm.com

Buy already picked pumpkins, enjoy a corn maze, and meet the animals. For the especially brave ones, the corn maze is haunted at night.

Meadowbrook Pumpkin Farm
2970 Mile View Rd.
West Bend, WI 53095
(262) 338-3649
http://www.meadowbrookfun.com

Pick your own pumpkins or buy already picked pumpkins. Also check out their corn maze, haunted corn maze, tractor-pulled hay rides, wagon rides, petting zoo, farm animals and more.

Prospect Hill Garden Center
19305 W. National Ave.
New Berlin, WI 53146
http://www.bloomssite.com

Enjoy a hayride to the pumpkin patch, a kids corn maze, petting zoo, lots of games for kids, face painting and food.

Schuett Farms LLC
W299 S6370 Hwy 83
Mukwonago, WI 53149
(262) 968-4348
http://www.schuettfarm.com

Pick your own pumpkins or buy already picked pumpkins, straw and cornstalk bundles. Also enjoy a corn maze and hayrides.

Swan Pumpkin Farm
5930 Highway H
Franksville, WI 53126
(262) 835-4885
http://www.thepumpkinfarm.com

Buy picked pumpkins, and enjoy a corn maze, tractor-pulled hayrides and more.

Witte's Vegetable Farm
10006 Bridge Rd.
Cedarburg, WI 53012
(262) 377-1423
http://www.wittesvegfarm.com

Pick your own pumpkins or buy already picked pumpkins, gourds and indian corn.

SPECIAL EVENTS

Retzer Howl-O-Ween: An Unhaunted Halloween Event
http://www.waukeshacounty.gov/defaultwc.aspx?id=39577

Each year in October, Retzer Nature Center hosts this family-friendly event recommended for children 10 and under. Enjoy an unhaunted barn dance, owl prowl hike, campfire stories and children's activity areas. Coming dressed in costumes is encouraged!

Boo at the Zoo & Halloween Spooktacular
http://www.zoosociety.org/events/boo.php

The Milwaukee County Zoo hosts special Fall events in October. In the past, Boo at the Zoo has included a haystack maze, bat exhibits, caramel apples, a pumpkin patch, light shows, spooky storytimes, and a haunted train ride. The Halloween Spooktacular features trick or treating throughout the zoo.

Do you have something to add? Email us at
miltownmoms@gmail.com.

CHAPTER 11: FAMILY MEMBERSHIPS
WHICH ONE IS WORTH IT FOR *YOUR* FAMILY?

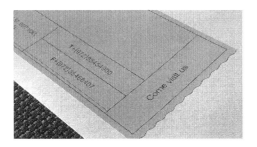

You've probably heard about at least one of the family memberships available to you at nearby attractions, but perhaps you've wondered if the price is really worth it. Here you can compare your options side by side and consider your own family's interests and hobbies to make the best decision.

BETTY BRINN CHILDREN'S MUSEUM

Regular price: $8.00/adult and child ages 1 & older (free for children ages 1 and younger)

Basic Family Membership = $75.00/year

What you get:
- Unlimited free admission for one year for two adults and all children in the household or grandchildren
- Member discount on parking in O'Donnell Park garage
- Discounts on events, parties and gift shop items
- Subscription to newsletter "Handprints."

Best for: Families with young children & families looking for somewhere to go on bad weather days. Betty Brinn offers additional programming that is free with admission, like Kids Yoga and Be a Maker programs.

DISCOVERY WORLD

Regular price:
Adult: $16.95
Child 3-17: $12.95
Child under 3: Free

Family Membership:
$85.00/year

What you get:
- 12 months of unlimited free admission for two adults and all children or grandchildren in household
- Free access to Kohl's Design It! Lab
- Quarterly Programs and Event Guide
- Subscription to to our eNewsletter
- Discount on workshops, camps, sleepovers, and theater programs
- Discounts in the Discovery World Innovation labs
- Invites to special member events
- Free deck tours on the S/V Denis Sullivan
- 10% discount in the Gift Shop and Cafe
- Members express entry desk
- Discounted parking in the Discovery World parking structure (except during lakefront special events)
- Reciprocal admission to over 250 science and technology centers around the globe

HARLEY-DAVIDSON MUSEUM

Regular Price: $18.00/adult $10.00/children ages 5-17

"Wrecking Crew" Family Membership: $75.00/year

What you get:
- Unlimited Museum visits for one year (two adults + two kids)
- H.O.G. Member recognition on your Museum membership card
- Optional guest card for designated second member or bring any guest each time you visit
- Your guests receive $4 off admission each time you visit
- The Backroad Chronicles – a pocket-sized Museum guide(new memberships only)
- Museum backpack

MILWAUKEE ART MUSEUM

Regular price: $17/Adult   Free for kids 12 & under

Family Membership: $85.00/year

What you get:
- Free admission for two adults and children 17 and under
- Two membership cards (designate two individuals or receive one guest card to bring a friend every time you visit)
- Unlimited access to feature exhibitions
- Free admission to Kohl's Art Generation Family Sundays, MAM After Dark, gallery talks, and lectures
- Invitations to Member Opening Celebration for feature exhibitions
- Reduced rates on classes, screenings, and pre-purchased parking passes
- The opportunity to join Museum support groups
- One-year subscription to our quarterly Member magazine
- 10% discount on Museum Store purchases, plus seasonal double discounts and Member Shopping Rewards throughout the year
- 10% discount at Café Calatrava

MILWAUKEE COUNTY ZOO PASS
*MILTOWNMOMS.COM PICK

Regular Price: Adult: $14.25 / Junior (age 3 to 12): $11.25
Child (2 and under): FREE

Basic Zoo Pass: $85.00/year

What you get:
- Free admission to the Milwaukee County Zoo for a full year
- Free or discounted admission to 150+ zoos and aquariums nation-wide
- Discounts on Zoological Society education classes and camps
- Members-only discounts on fundraising events
- Wild Things newsletter – six times per year
- Members-only events
- Alive magazine
- Members-only discounts in the Zoo's gift shops
- Exclusive members-only discounts on the Oceans of Fun, Inc. interactive programs; Sea Lion Splash and Aquatic Adventures, & members-only field trips to other zoos, aquariums and places of interest.

Something to consider: A family of four only has to visit the zoo twice for this pass to be worth the price. The Zoo Pass Plus includes parking.

Best for: Families with animal lovers & families looking for outdoor fun.

MILWAUKEE PUBLIC MUSEUM

Regular price: $15.00/adult
$11.00/child 3-12 years old

Basic Family Membership =
$99.00/year

What you get:
- Unlimited free admission for one year for two adults and all children 17 & under
- Free admission to more than 300 museums worldwide
- Free evening member events, such as Halloween Hauntings & MPM Inside Out
- Free Clue Crew Kids Club membership
- Free subscription to member newsletter & monthly eNewsletter

- Discounts on special exhibitions & members-only viewings
- Discounts on parking & purchases at MPM shops/cafe
- Discounts on Museum camps, lectures & other public programs
- Free stroller or wheelchair rental (one per visit)

SCHLITZ AUDUBON NATURE CENTER

Regular price: $6.00/adult $4.00/child

Family Membership: $60.00/year

What you get:
- Unlimited, FREE admission to the Center all-year long
- Subscription to the Center's bi-monthly newsletter
- Discounted fees on all programs and classes
- A 10% discount in our Nature Store
- Admission to more than 140 nature centers in the United States and Canada
- Priority registration for our nature preschool and summer nature adventure camps
- Invitations to exclusive members-only events
- Membership in the Schlitz Audubon Bird Club

URBAN ECOLOGY CENTER
*MILTOWNMOMS.COM PICK

Family Membership: $45.00/year

What you get:
- Free access to outdoor adventure equipment including canoes, kayaks, bikes, camping equipment, cross country skis, snowshoes, sleds, ice skates, gardening tools, and more for up to three days completely free at all three of our branches
- Discounts on public programs & camps

Best for: Nature-loving families throughout the Milwaukee area.

Do you have something to add? Email us at
miltownmoms@gmail.com.

CHAPTER 12: INDOOR PLAYGROUNDS

(Sprecher soda at Bounce Milwaukee)

On days when Milwaukee weather makes you want to stay indoors, but your kids have energy that needs to be spent, consider one of these indoor playgrounds to lift everyone's spirits. They offer inflatables, play-sets, arcade games, laser tag, indoor climbing walls, and more.

The Big Backyard
2857 S. 160th St.
New Berlin, WI 53151
(262) 797-9117
http://www.thebigbackyardwi.com

Designed for kids 0-8, huge play equipment, riding toys, balls, playhouses, infant toys, and more. Space for parties and special events available.

Bounce Milwaukee
2801 S. 5th Ct.
Milwaukee, WI 53207
(414) 312-4357
http://www.bouncemilwaukee.com

The state's only 360 degree laser tag arena, rock climbing, inflatable sports arena, adrenaline zone and vintage video games. They also do birthday parties. Get $10.00 off your next birthday party at Bounce Milwaukee with coupon code MILTOWNMOMS,

Bounce Realm
4595 S 27th St.
Greenfield, WI 53221
(414) 281-8000
http://www.childpartiesgreenfield.com

Indoor, party place for kids 12 & under. Bounce houses, moon walks, kids party games, token-operated games like skeet ball & prizes.

Chasing Tales
7265 S. 1st St.
Oak Creek, WI 53154
(414) 254-PLAY
http://chasingtalesforkids.com

Walkers, tricycles, ball games, life size checkers, and varied playground equipment encourages physical movement and the development of gross motor skills. The role play area allows children to act out different scenarios in a household setting, grocery store, puppet theater, and dress up theater. There are also various construction materials for children to use their imaginations to create different structures. A puzzle and library corner enables children to work on quieter skills such as spatial reasoning and early literacy skills.

Family Tree Haus
5080 W. Ashland Way
Franklin, WI 53132
(414) 423-1707
http://familytreehaus.com

5,000 square ft. indoor playground with distinct play areas filled with age appropriate playground equipment for tots up to 5, and older kids 5 to 10. Birthday parties available.

Flabbergast
W248 N5250 Executive Dr.
Sussex, WI 53089
262-246-0711
http://www.flabbergastfun.com

Open play, all day, every day! Brand-new, state-of-the-art, clean, and secure indoor entertainment facility for birthday party fun & indoor play.

Helium Trampoline Park
16235 W. Beloit Rd.
New Berlin, WI 53151
(262) 777-2100
http://heliumtrampolinepark.com

Trampolines, basketball, foam pit & rock wall! Walk-in hours and birthday parties.

Infinite Gymnastics
8989 N. 55th St.
Brown Deer, WI 53223
(414) 371-9520
http://www.infinitegymnastics.com

Circuits, mazes, hills and caves, trampolines, loose foam pits, and birthday parties!

Jumping Country
1235 Dakota Dr.
Grafton, WI 53024
(262) 377-6700
http://jumpingcountry.com

Giant slides, obstacle courses, competitions, inflatable sport games, & more. Three private party rooms for small or large parties.

Jump Zone
6544 S. 108th St.
Franklin, WI 53132
(414) 409-7610
http://www.jumpzoneparty.com

Massive, themed inflatable slides, obstacle courses and bounce houses, interactive games, toddler activities and more.

Just 4 Fun
2100 Washington St.
Grafton, WI 53024
(262) 375-4507
http://just4funplayland.com/wp_j4f/

Large indoor playground, bikes, toys, cafe and more!

Kids in Motion
14135 W. Greenfield Ave.
New Berlin, WI 53151
(262) 649-3144
http://www.kidsinmotionwi.com

Indoor soft play area, parachutes, slides, tunnels, laser tag, stage, arts & crafts, train room, science & conservation room, grocery room, music room and game room.

LaFleurs Gymnastics Academy
189 Kleinmann Dr
Germantown, WI 53022
(262) 255-9700
http://www.lafleursgym.com

Open gyms throughout the week featuring three huge inflatables! Birthday parties available.

Monkey Joe's
2040 W Blue Mound Rd.   4237 Green Bay Rd.
Waukesha, WI   #102, Kenosha, WI
(262) 549-3866   (262) 764-3866

http://www.monkeyjoes.com

Wall-to-wall inflatable slides, jumps, and obstacle courses. Birthday parties available.

Pump it Up
195 N. Janacek Rd
Brookfield, WI 53045-6100
(262) 780-1010
http://www.pumpitupparty.com

Play areas packed with gigantic inflatables!

Skyzone Indoor Trampoline Park
W229 N1420 Westwood Dr.
Waukesha, WI 53186
262-696-1600
http://www.skyzone.com

OTHER INDOOR PLAY IDEAS

Barnes & Noble
Locations in Glendale, Greenfield, Tosa & Brookfield

Barnes & Noble kids' areas offer train tables, legos, reading areas and more.

Playshore
Bayshore Town Center Food Court

Southridge Mall Kids' Play Area
Greendale

CHAPTER 13: LIBRARIES
NOT JUST STORY TIME!

Libraries are a rich source for high-quality fun that is completely free for families. They offer family matinees, lego clubs, yoga for kids, kid-friendly music, game nights, tutoring, free wifi access and so much more. Find libraries near you, or venture out and explore a new one using this comprehensive guide.

MILWAUKEE PUBLIC LIBRARY BRANCHES

Atkinson
1960 W. Atkinson Ave.
Milwaukee, WI 53209
(414) 286-3000
http://www.mpl.org/hours_locations/atkinson.php

This library boasts unique architecture highlighted by a beamed, cathedral vaulted ceiling, woodwork and modern stained glass windows. The branch features 22 desktop computers for public use, 28 laptops for use inside the library, free Wi-Fi for all visitors, a meeting room, a study room, a free Scanner with capability to email or save documents to a flash drive, a color printer, a plentiful Urban Fiction collection, homework help after school with teacher, free computer classes for city residents & drop-in job search and resume help.

Bay View
2566 S. Kinnickinnic Ave.
Milwaukee, WI 53207
(414) 286-3000
http://www.mpl.org/hours_locations/bay_view.php

This open, bright library houses three mosaic maps in the linoleum floor of the lobby, one representing Bay View at the time of settlement in 1832; another from 1900, when a steel mill on the lakefront spurred the community's growth; the third showing the area as it is today. The branch features weekly story times for young children, monthly Book Club discussions, monthly knitting groups, 22 desktop computers for public use, 18 laptops for use inside the library, free Wi-Fi for all visitors, homework help after school with teacher, free computer classes for city residents, drop-in job search and resume help, a public meeting room a free Scanner with capability to email or save documents to a flash drive, and a color printer.

Capitol
3969 N. 74th St.
Milwaukee, WI 53216
(414) 286-3000
http://www.mpl.org/hours_locations/capitol.php

Capitol's collection includes popular materials such as fiction, magazines, DVDs, music CDs and audiobooks. Popular programs are preschool story time and 'Teacher in the Library'. Capitol Library is open on Sundays during the school year (October-April). The library offers WiFi, laptops for in-library use and two community meeting rooms.

Center Street
2727 W. Fond du Lac Ave.
Milwaukee, WI 53210
(414) 286-3000
http://www.mpl.org/hours_locations/center_street.php

The Center Street branch features a children's story corner illuminated by a sky-light ceiling, small and large group meeting rooms, media and adult tutoring rooms, and the African American Wall of Fame and Children Mural created by Reynaldo Hernandez. The works of 20 other local artists are on display." The technology center project greatly increases public access to computers, online resources and computer training at Center Street Library.

Central
814 W. Wisconsin Ave.
Milwaukee, WI 53233
(414) 286-3000
http://www.mpl.org/hours_locations/central.php

Conduct research school, browse the shelves for classics and bestsellers, and use computers to access information. The vast collections of the Central Library serves as a resource library for the entry library system and for the state. Central Library has been designated a landmark by the Milwaukee Historic Preservation Commission and is listed on the National Register of Historic Places.

Central library hosts family programs every Saturday at 10:30 a.m. in the Central Library Betty Brinn Children's Room. They also host special family events throughout the year. Check their website or the MiltownMoms.com Event Calendar for details.

East
2430 N. Murray Ave.
Milwaukee, WI 53211
http://www.mpl.org/hours_locations/east.php

Milwaukee residents will soon have a new East Branch of the Milwaukee Public Library. Construction is now underway on a multi-use development on the site - The Standard @ East Library - a 5-story building housing a new 16,000 square foot library, 99 apartments with underground parking, surface parking for library patrons and a retail space adjacent to the library on the first floor. The Standard @ East Library is being developed by HSI, Inc. and designed by Engberg Anderson. For more information contact (414) 227-0900 or visit www.thestandardmke.com/.

Forest Home
1432 W. Forest Home Ave.
Milwaukee, WI 53204
http://www.mpl.org/hours_locations/forest_home.php

Forest Home has a large collection of Spanish language materials for adults and children, an impressive Native Americal collections, and offers computer classes in English and Spanish in a new computer lab. A drop-in tutoring program serves adults and students in the community. Forest Home also offers a wide variety of children's and teen programming including the popular Teacher in the Library program.

Martin Luther King
310 W. Locust St.
Milwaukee, WI 53212
http://www.mpl.org/hours_locations/mlking.php

Martin Luther King Library features 21 computers with internet access and Microsoft Word, Powerpoint and Excel, an extensive African American Collection, DVD movies and books for all ages, free computer classes for adults, a large meeting space, and a collection of permanent art, some pertaining to Dr. King, and a unique accordion book by Amos Paul Kennedy, Jr. which contains Dr. King's most noted quotations and adinkra symbols associated with the Ashanti people.

Mill Road
6431 N. 76th St.
Milwaukee, WI 53223
http://www.mpl.org/hours_locations/mill_road.php

Mill Road offers WiFi, laptops for in-library use, and meeting room space for community groups. In addition to popular materials, DVDs, music CDs and magazines, Mill Road offers adult drop-in tutoring and free computer classes.

Tippecanoe
3912 S. Howell Ave.
Milwaukee, WI 53207
http://www.mpl.org/hours_locations/tippecanoe.php

The Tippecanoe library features a Guido Brink sculpture, a suspended three-color metal sculpture inspired by the Native-American Indian name of the library. In 2014, Tippecanoe will underwent a complete renovation of the interior of the building.

Tippecanoe Branch features weekly story times for young children, a monthly book club discussion, a computer lab and laptops, free Wi-Fi, free computer classes for city residents, drop-in job search and resume help, a meeting room, a free scanner and a color printer.

Villard Square
5190 N. 35th St.
Milwaukee, WI 53209
http://www.mpl.org/hours_locations/villard_square.php

The Villard Square Branch is a mixed-use development that includes a Milwaukee Public Library branch on the first floor, with 47 apartment homes on three stories above for families where grandparents are the primary caregivers for their grandchildren.

The library includes more than 50 desktop and laptop computers for users, community meeting and study rooms, children's and teen areas, and self-checkout stations. An on-site parking lot for 32 cars is included. Nestled in the northwest side of the city, Villard Square Branch serves a vibrant multicultural neighborhood.

Washington Park
2121 N. Sherman Blvd.
Milwaukee, WI 53208
http://www.mpl.org/hours_locations/washington_park.php

This 20,000-square-foot library is the City of Milwaukee's largest neighborhood library. Named for the park it borders, the library offers computers for public use, a community meeting space, a large area for children and young adults; an expansive collection of books, videos, CDs and DVDs, and an adult tutoring program.

Zablocki

3501 W. Oklahoma Ave.
Milwaukee, WI 53215
http://www.mpl.org/hours_locations/zablocki.php

Zablocki Library houses a large popular materials collection and offers a wide variety of programs including preschool story hours, family events and computers for public use.

SUBURBAN LIBRARIES

Brookfield Public Library

1900 N. Calhoun Rd.
Brookfield, WI 53005
(262) 782-4140
http://www.ci.brookfield.wi.us/index.aspx?NID=38

Lego club, children's book club, kid-friendly music and more!

Cudahy Family Library

500 Library Dr.
Cudahy, Wisconsin 53110
(414) 769-2244
http://www.cudahyfamilylibrary.org

Story time for babies, toddlers and preschoolers, LEGO Club, Art Club and special events throughout the year.

Franklin Public Library

9151 W. Loomis Rd.
Franklin, WI 53132
(414) 425-8214
http://www.mcfls.org/franklin/

Franklin Public Library offers year-round programming for all ages. Programs include Waddlers and Walkers (Ages 23 months and younger), Tales for Twos (Age 2), Preschool Pretend and Play (3-5 years old), Music and Motion (2-5 years old), and Rhyming to Read (2-5 years old). While visiting, don't miss their reading and learning tree, their toy lending library and their vacation backpacks.

North Shore Library

6800 N. Port Washington Rd.
Milwaukee, WI 53217
(414) 351-3461
http://www.mcfls.org/northshorelibrary/

North Shore Library serves Bayside, Fox Point, Glendale and River Hills. It offers a variety of children's programming all year round.

Oak Creek Public Library

8620 S. Howell Ave.
Oak Creek, WI 53154
(414) 764-4400
http://www.oakcreeklibrary.org

Oak Creek Public Library offers story-times and programming for all ages year-round.

Shorewood Public Library

3920 N. Murray Ave.
Shorewood, WI
(414) 847-2670
http://www.shorewoodlibrary.org

Shorewood Public Library offers year-round story-times, crafts, computer classes, tween programming, and more!

St. Francis Public Library

4230 S. Nicholson Ave.
St Francis, WI 53235
(414) 481-7323
http://www.stfrancislibrary.org

St. Francis Library offers preschool and toddler story-times, special events, and reading programs throughout the year.

Wauwatosa Public Library

7635 W. North Ave.
Wauwatosa, WI 53213
(414) 471-8485

http://wauwatosalibrary.org

Rhyme time, story times and special events for all ages.

West Allis Public Library
7421 W. National Ave.
West Allis, WI 53214
(414) 302-8503
http://www.westalliswi.gov/library

Lego Club, preschool and infant story times, family programs and more.

Whitefish Bay Public Library
5420 N. Marlborough Dr.
Milwaukee, WI 53217
http://www.wfblibrary.org

Story-times, family movies, tween programming, book clubs, and more.

Do you have something to add? Email us at
miltownmoms@gmail.com.

CHAPTER 14: MUSEUMS

(Children's Section in the Harley-Davidson Museum)

Think museums are quiet and stuffy? Think again! The Milwaukee area boasts a wide variety of kid-friendly museums that enable children to explore science, technology, history, motorcycles, dinosaurs, and more. So, what are you waiting for? Get out and explore!

ART MUSEUMS

Lynden Sculpture Garden

2145 W. Brown Deer Rd.
Milwaukee, WI 53217
(414) 446-8794
http://lyndensculpturegarden.org

The Lynden Sculpture Garden offers a unique experience of art in nature through its collection of more than 50 monumental sculptures sited across 40 acres of park, lake and woodland. They offer a monthly Tuesdays in the Garden program for small children and weekly art drop-in programs for older kids.

Milwaukee Art Museum

700 Art Museum Dr.
Milwaukee, WI 53202
(414) 224-3200
http://mam.org

Kids under 12 are always admitted for free at the world-class Milwaukee Art Museum. It's also free to everyone on the first Thursday of every month. (Thanks, Target! Just one more reason why I love thee.)

Younger children will enjoy **Story Time in the Galleries** every Saturday at 10:30 a.m. Children sit beneath one of the paintings in the Gallery and enjoy a story and a craft that relates to it. They can also get creative at the **Play Date with Art**, a monthly program that includes a themed craft and singing time.

The whole family can take advantage of **ArtPacks**, which are filled with self-guided activities such as sketch-packs, scavenger hunts, and iPod Touch Tours. You can also visit **Kohl's Art Generation Open Studio,** open every Saturday and Sunday from 10:00-4:00, to create a themed art project to take home. And don't miss the high-tech, interactive **Kohl's Art Generation Lab** where you can explore what happens behind the scenes at the Museum.

Finally, the Museum hosts **Family Sundays** five times a year, where families can participate in hands-on art activities and enjoy interactive performances, family tours & visiting artists.

Be sure to check out their **Youth Studio Classes** (after school) and **Summer Art Camps** if you're child is artistically inclined (or, I suppose, if they're not.)

Museum of Wisconsin Art (MOWA)
205 Veterans Ave.
West Bend, WI 53095
(262) 334-9638
http://www.wisconsinart.org

MOWA is the only museum in the world that is dedicated to collecting and maintaining works from Wisconsin. They offer themed Studio Saturdays every month for families to enjoy, as well as a monthly art program designed just for babies. They also offer Junior Masters studio projects designed for older kids to explore various art techniques.

NATURAL HISTORY AND SCIENCE MUSEUMS

Dinosaur Discovery Museum
5608 Tenth Ave.
Kenosha, WI
(262) 653-4450
http://www.kenosha.org/wp-dinosaur/

The main gallery of the Dinosaur Discovery Museum is a primer on dinosaurs – what they were, how we know they existed, what they looked like, how they behaved, how and why they were alike and different, and what happened to them. The dinosaur skeletons in the main gallery are casts of actual dinosaur fossil bones. Each dinosaur is labeled with information about the species. Panels on the gallery wall answer the most-asked questions about dinosaurs. You can listen to the environmental and animal sounds in the exhibit gallery. Step back into the Mesozoic era with outdoors sounds in different terrains and weather conditions during the Age of Dinosaurs.

Milwaukee Public Museum
800 W. Wells St.
Milwaukee, WI 53233
(414) 278-2728
http://www.mpm.edu

One of the premier natural history and science facilities, the museum is world-renowned for its exhibits, collections, & ongoing scientific research. Milwaukee County Residents receive free admission on Thursdays and Milwaukee County Residents receive a $2.00 discount on admission every day.

North Point Lighthouse
2650 N. Wahl Ave.
Milwaukee, WI 53211
(414) 332-6754
http://northpointlighthouse.org

The North Point Lighthouse Museum offers a wide variety of artifacts about Milwaukee's famous lighthouse and its keepers. Visitors can also see exhibits about the heritage, culture and role that Milwaukee has played in the regional maritime activities of the Great Lakes. The Museum has a diverse collection of artwork, artifacts, documents and educational materials. Our collection is growing thanks to the generosity of our keepers' descendants, other maritime museums, historical societies and friends. Climb the tower for a spectacular view of Lake Michigan, Milwaukee & Lake Park.

Waukesha County Museum

101 W. Main St.
Waukesha, WI 53186
(262) 521-2859
http://www.waukeshacountymuseum.org

The Waukesha County Museum is an educational and cultural resource for the area, while preserving and sharing its county history. They provide family programming all year round and day camps during the Summer.

LIVING HISTORY MUSEUMS

Old World Wisconsin
W372 S9727 Wisconsin 67
Eagle, WI 53119
(262) 594-6301
http://oldworldwisconsin.wisconsinhistory.org

Old World Wisconsin is a 600-acre open-air museum located near Eagle, Wisconsin. It portrays housing and the daily life of immigrants in 19th century Wisconsin. It is the largest outdoor museum of rural life in the United States. They offer family-friendly programming, events and activities throughout the year.

Pioneer Village
4880 County Road I
Saukville, WI 53080
(262) 377-4510
http://www.ochs.co.ozaukee.wi.us

Pioneer Village is a living history museum with 17 buildings from the 1840-1907 era. The homes are fully furnished. Barns and outbuildings plus the original Cedarburg Railroad Depot has been relocated and restored here in a unique rural setting. Special family-friendly events happen throughout the summer. They are open Saturdays and Sundays from Noon-5:00 p.m. from Memorial Day-Mid-October. The last tour runs at 4:00 p.m. each day.

Trimborn Farm
8881 W. Grange Ave.
Greendale, WI 53129
(414) 273-8288
http://www.milwaukeehistory.net/historic-sites-2/trimborn-farm/

Trimborn Farm is the only Milwaukee County Park with a historic theme. Nine original structures on the remaining 7.5 acres of land comprise the heart of the original estate.

OTHER

Betty Brinn Children's Museum
929 E. Wisconsin Ave.
Milwaukee, WI 53202
(414) 390-5437
https://www.bbcmkids.org

Hands-on play and interactive learning for kids ten and under and their grown-ups!

Harley-Davidson Museum
400 W. Canal St.
Milwaukee, WI 53201
(414) 287-2789
http://www.harley-davidson.com/content/h-d/en_US/home/museum.html

The Harley-Davidson Museum offers 12 "can't-miss" family-friendly exhibits.

Mitchell Gallery of Flight
5300 S. Howell Ave.
Milwaukee, WI 53207
(414) 747-4503
http://mitchellgallery.org

This non-profit aviation museum is located inside Milwaukee's General Mitchell International Airport. Check out aviation artifacts, memorabilia & photographs.

Do you have something to add? Email us at
miltownmoms@gmail.com.

CHAPTER 15: MUSIC LESSONS AND PERFORMANCES

Got music? Milwaukee is home to several organizations that provide music lessons for all ages and abilities, as well as concerts and musical enrichment experiences featuring some of the finest musicians in the region.

Festival City Symphony

3480 W. Bradley Rd.
Milwaukee, WI 53209
(414) 365-8861
http://www.festivalcitysymphony.org

Festival City Symphony offers casual, family-friendly classical concerts for all ages such as Pajama Jamborees and affordable, family-friendly Symphony Sunday performances.

Milwaukee Youth Symphony Orchestra

325 W. Walnut St.
Milwaukee, WI 53212
(414) 267-2906
http://www.myso.org/newsite/

Milwaukee Youth Symphony Orchestra (MYSO) is one of the most successful and respected youth orchestra programs in the nation, regularly recognized for its artistic excellence. MYSO offers more than 25 ensemble options, ranging from symphony and string orchestras, to jazz and steel pan bands, all providing high quality musical experiences to students at various skill levels.

Music Together

Various locations
http://musictogether.com

Music Together is an internationally recognized early childhood music and movement program for children from birth through age 7 and the grownups who love them.

Wisconsin Conservatory of Music

1584 N. Prospect Ave.
Milwaukee, WI 53202
(414) 276-5760
http://www.wcmusic.org

The Conservatory offers music lessons and camps for all ages, as well as concerts, recitals and other special events.

Music and Me
https://www.bbcmkids.org

Check out this Music & Me class, free with museum admission, at Betty Brinn Children's Museum. Takes place many Fridays at 10:30 a.m. Check the calendar for exact dates.

Sharon Lynne Wilson Center for Arts
http://www.wilson-center.com

This arts center offers youth and family music classes starting at age one. Their music classes are offered through the Wisconsin Conservatory of Music.

Do you have something to add? Email us at
miltownmoms@gmail.com.

CHAPTER 16: NATURE CENTERS

(The Tropical Dome at the Mitchell Park Domes)

One of the best parts about living in Milwaukee is soaking up the four seasons in all their glory. The area's nature centers are host to indigenous wildlife, fantastic educators, and in some case, exotic species. Between free family hikes, 3D planetariums, and creative programming for all ages, exploring nature in Milwaukee has never been more easy and fun.

Boerner Botanical Gardens

9400 Boerner Dr.
Hales Corners, WI 53130
(414) 525-5650
http://boernerbotanicalgardens.org

The Boerner Botanical Gardens, an internationally renowned horticultural showplace in the Milwaukee County Parks, offers gardeners, plant lovers and students the opportunity to take in the colors and scents of a variety of collections.

Growing Power

5500 W. Silver Spring Dr.
Milwaukee, WI
(414) 527-1930
http://growingpower.org

This historic two-acre farm is the last remaining farm and greenhouse operation in the City of Milwaukee. Since 1999, our Community Food Center has provided a wonderful space for hands-on activities, large-scale demonstration projects, and for growing a myriad of plants, vegetables, and herbs. In a space no larger than a small supermarket live some 20,000 plants and vegetables, thousands of fish, and a livestock inventory of chickens, goats, ducks, rabbits, and bees.

Lamm Gardens

2708 Sherman Rd.
Jackson, WI 53037
(262) 677-3010
http://www.lammscape.com

Lammscape's beautifully landscaped grounds are open to the public for free events throughout the season. Check out their "Trees and Trains" event and their "Little Lambs" kids activities.

Lynden Sculpture Gardens

2145 W. Brown Deer Rd.
Milwaukee, WI 53217
(414) 446-8794
http://lyndensculpturegarden.org

The Lynden Sculpture Garden offers a unique experience of art in nature through its collection of more than 50 monumental sculptures sited across 40 acres of park, lake and woodland. They offer a monthly Tuesdays in the Garden program for small children and weekly art drop-in programs for older kids.

Havenwoods State Forest Nature Center
6141 N. Hopkins St.
Milwaukee, WI 53209
(414) 527-0232
http://dnr.wi.gov/topic/parks/name/havenwoods/

Havenwoods houses small critters in their Nature Center and offers free family programming throughout the week and on weekends. Programs include nature-themed story times, family hikes and up-cycled crafts.

Hawthorn Glen
1130 N. 60th St.
Milwaukee, WI 53208
(414) 647-6050
http://www.milwaukeerecreation.net/hawthorn-glen/

Hawthorn Glen is a 23-acre nature center featuring steep bluffs, flood-plain hardwood forest, spring-fed wetland, and a restored prairie. Visitors to this urban nature center can explore five different habitats interconnected by a trail system. The public is welcome to utilize the facility and the well-marked ¾ mile self-guided nature trail in the evenings or on weekends (the lower trail is mostly blacktopped and ADA accessible). Many seasonal programs are offered on the weekends.

Kompost Kids
http://www.kompostkids.com

Kompost Kids educates about the benefits of composting. They hold a family-friendly composting demonstration every Saturday, and host other fun events throughout the year.

Lion's Den Gorge Nature Preserve
511 High Bluff Dr.
Grafton, Wisconsin 53024
(262) 284-8257

Lion's Den Gorge Nature Preserve represents one of the last stretches of undeveloped bluff land along the Lake Michigan shoreline, from Mequon up to Port Washington. Over 1/2 mile of 90 to 100 foot bluffs look out onto Lake Michigan, offering tremendous viewing opportunities for residents and visitors. Stroll across bridges over the gorge or down the gorge stairways to walk along the Lake Mighican shoreline. This 73 acre park offers plenty of hiking trails, boardwalks through the wetlands, picnic areas, scenic views, and restrooms.

Mitchell Park Horticultural Conservatory - "The Domes"
524 S. Layton Blvd.
Milwaukee, WI 53215
(414) 257-5611
http://www.milwaukeedomes.org

Experience a desert oasis, a tropical jungle and special floral gardens, all in one afternoon!

Retzer Nature Center
S14 W 28167 Madison St.
Waukesha, WI 53188
(262) 896-8007
http://www.waukeshacounty.gov/defaultwc.aspx?id=39577

Schlitz Audubon Nature Center
1111 E. Brown Deer Rd.
Bayside, WI 53217
(414) 352-2880
http://www.sanc.org

Urban Ecology Center
Locations in Riverside Park, Menomonee Valley, Washington Park
http://urbanecologycenter.org

Wehr Nature Center
9701 W. College Ave.
Franklin, WI 53132
(414) 425-8550
http://www.friendsofwehr.org

CHAPTER 17: BEACH GUIDE

Did you know there are nine public beaches in Milwaukee County along the beautiful shores of Lake Michigan? This guide lists them in order form north to south. It might be fun to visit each one at least once this Summer.

Doctor's Park
1870 E. Fox Ln.
Fox Point, WI 53217

Located north of downtown Milwaukee in Fox Point, Doctors Park boasts nearly 50 acres of beauty on a bluff. Above, you'll find a playground and practice fields. Take a paved trail, stairs, or a dirt trail down to the beach.

Klode Park
5900 N. Lake Dr.
Whitefish Bay, WI 53217

Located north of downtown Milwaukee in Whitefish Bay, Klode Park offers breathtaking views, a winding path down to the beach, and a playground for the kiddos.

Big Bay Park
5000 N. Palisades Rd.
Whitefish Bay, WI 53217

Another pleasant beach tucked away in Whitefish Bay, Big Bay Park features a path to the beach and a scenic overlook of the lake.

Atwater Beach
East Capitol and North Lake Drive Shorewood, WI

Head down the steep set of stairs to enjoy the open area to run and play. Don't miss the impressive sculpture by Spanish artist Jaume Plensa of a contemplative man overlooking the beach.

Bradford Beach
2400 N. Lincoln Memorial Dr.
Milwaukee, WI 53211

Defining the classic Beach Day in Milwaukee, Bradford Beach offers volleyball, upbeat crowds and custard at North Point Snack Shack.

McKinley Beach
1750 N. Lincoln Memorial Dr.
Milwaukee, WI 53202

Grab a Berry Booster smoothie from Alterra on the Lake and head north to

McKinley Beach. It's less crowded than Bradford Beach and has a playground to wear out the little ones.

South Shore Beach
2900 S. Superior St.
Milwaukee, WI 53207

Nestled in Bay View, this beach offers beautiful views of South Shore Yacht Club, a playground and a large park with picnic tables and a sand volleyball court.

Grant Park Beach
100 S. Hawthorne Ave.
South Milwaukee, WI 53172

Head to South Milwaukee to hike the Seven Bridges Trail of Grant Park, and end with a dip in the lake.

Bender Park Beach
4503 E. Ryan Rd.
Oak Creek, WI

One of the County's newest parks, Bender Park features a harbor and a boat launch. There are some rumors that it's haunted, so proceed with caution!

Do you have something to add? Email us at
miltownmoms@gmail.com.

CHAPTER 18: STATE PARKS
TWELVE WITHIN ONE HOUR OF MILWAUKEE

If city life begins to overwhelm you and your family and you need to reconnect with nature, consider visiting one of the twelve state parks within just one hour of Milwaukee. You can hike, swim, canoe, or just pack a picnic and enjoy the day.

Aztalan State Park
N6200 Hwy Q
Lake Mills, WI 53549
(920) 648-8774
http://dnr.wi.gov/topic/parks/name/aztalan/

Aztalan State Park is a National Historic Landmark and contains one of Wisconsin's most important archaeological sites. It showcases an ancient Middle-Mississippian village that thrived between A.D. 1000 and 1300. The people who settled Aztalan built large, flat-topped pyramidal mounds and a stockade around their village. Portions of the stockade and two mounds have been reconstructed in the park.

Big Foot Beach State Park
1452 S. Wells St.
Lake Geneva, WI 53147
(262) 248-2528
http://dnr.wi.gov/topic/parks/name/bigfoot/

This 271-acre park on the shore of Geneva Lakeoffers wooded campsites, a sand beach, 6.5 miles of hiking trails, and picnic areas.

Glacial Drumlin State Trail
810 College Ave.
Waukesha, WI 53188
http://glacialdrumlin.com

Running between Wisconsin's two largest urban areas, this trail stretches for 52 miles through farmlands and glacial topography. The trail travels through 10 small towns from Cottage Grove to Waukesha. The trail is on an abandoned rail corridor, except for a 1.5-mile section northeast of Jefferson, between State Highway 26 and County Highway Y, which uses public roads as the trail route.

Harrington Beach State Park
531 County Road D
Belgium, WI 53004
(262) 285-3015
http://dnr.wi.gov/topic/parks/name/harrington/

Harrington Beach State Park has more than a mile of beach along Lake Michigan. This 715-acre park also features a white cedar and hardwood swamp, old field grasslands with restored wetland ponds and a scenic limestone quarry lake. Camp, sunbathe, picnic, hike, bird watch, fish or practice astronomy. An observatory is open to the public for monthly viewings.

Havenwoods State Forest
6141 N. Hopkins St.
Milwaukee, WI 53209
http://dnr.wi.gov/topic/parks/name/havenwoods/

Havenwoods State Forest is Wisconsin's only urban state forest, featuring 237 acres of grasslands, woods and wetlands in the city of Milwaukee. Hike, run, bike and watch wildlife on over six miles of trails. Explore one of the four ponds, stroll over the 120-foot bridge or find a bench to sit and relax outdoors.

Kettle Moraine State Forest Lapham Peak Unit
W 329 N 846
Delafield, WI 53018
(262) 646-3025
http://dnr.wi.gov/topic/parks/name/lapham/

The Kettle Moraine and Lapham Peak were formed 10,000 years ago when a glacier covered much of Wisconsin. Lapham Peak's glaciated topography provides excellent hiking, backpacking, and cross-country skiing on lighted trails. Climb a 45-foot observation tower atop the highest point in Waukesha County (1,233 feet above sea level).

Kettle Moraine State Forest Northern Unit
N2875 State Road 67
Campbellsport, WI
(920) 533-8322
http://dnr.wi.gov/topic/parks/name/kmn/

The Kettle Moraine Northern Unit is comprised of about 30,000 acres stretching 30 miles across Sheboygan, Fond du Lac and Washington Counties. Enjoy hiking, canoeing, kayaking, paddle boating, & more!

Kettle Moraine State Forest Pike Lake Unit
3544 Kettle Moraine Rd.
Hartford, WI 53086
(262) 670-3400
http://dnr.wi.gov/topic/parks/name/pikelake/

The Pike Lake Unit of the Kettle Moraine State Forest is in the middle of the Kettle Moraine, a strip of glacial landforms which extends through southeastern Wisconsin to Lake Winnebago. The forest is named after the 522-acre, spring-fed kettle: Pike Lake. Powder Hill provides the opportunity for a great hike and view. Visitors can enjoy camping, swimming, hiking, fishing, picnicking, and much more within the forest.

Kettle Moraine State Forest Southern Unit
S58 W35820 Co Road Zz
Dousman, WI
(262) 594-6200
http://dnr.wi.gov/topic/parks/name/kms/

More than 22,000 acres of glacial hills, kettles, lakes, prairie restoration sites, pine woods and hardwood forests can be found in the Southern Unit, making this a popular area for a wide variety of visitors. The Forest is 30 miles long, extending from the village of Dousman, almost to the city of Whitewater. The forest headquarters is 3 miles west of the village of Eagle on State Highway 59.

Kohler-Andrae State Park
1020 Beach Park Ln.
Sheboygan, WI 53081
(920) 451-4080
http://dnr.wi.gov/topic/parks/name/kohlerandrae/

Kohler-Andrae State Park in Sheboygan, Wisconsin, is the home of majestic sand dunes, miles of golden beach, shimmering blue Lake Michigan water, whispering pines, an abundance of wildlife, and recreational activities for everyone. Kohler-Andrae State Park is one of the last natural preserves along the Lake Michigan shore, and is open for everyone to explore and enjoy.

Lakeshore State Park
500 N. Harbor Dr.
Milwaukee, WI 53202
(414) 274-4281
http://dnr.wi.gov/topic/parks/name/lakeshore/

In the heart of downtown Milwaukee, Lakeshore State Park provides a unique urban oasis with recreational and educational opportunities geared to the urban population. Lakeshore State Park offers great views of the city and Lake Michigan and has a reservable, overnight boat slip.

Richard Bong State Recreation Area
Kansasville, WI 53139
http://dnr.wi.gov/topic/parks/name/richardbong

Once designated to be a jet fighter base, Richard Bong State Recreation Area is fittingly named after Major Richard I. Bong, a Poplar, WI native who was America's leading air ace during World War II. The air base was abandoned three days before concrete was to be poured for a 12,500-foot runway. Local citizens had the foresight to protect this open space for future generations.

Do you have something to add? Email us at
miltownmoms@gmail.com.

CHAPTER 19: PLAYGROUPS

(Enjoy the yellow slide and rocking horse in Bay View Community Center's playroom.)

If you find yourself home with your young children and you'd like to find an opportunity for them to socialize with other kids in a stimulating environment, explore our favorite playgroups around town.

Bay View Community Center
1320 E. Oklahoma Ave.
Milwaukee, Wisconsin 53207
(414) 482-1000
http://www.bayviewcenter.org

Playgroups meet every day of the week! Just $1.00 per visit. Join us in our family friendly children's room with fun toys for the whole family. Ride the horse, slide down the big yellow slide, dress-up like a fireman or play with our wide variety of toys. Your family will have the opportunity to socialize with other families and enjoy snack and juice for the kids and coffee for the parents.

COA Youth & Family Center - Riverwest
909 E. North Ave.
Milwaukee, WI 53212
(414) 263- 8383
http://www.coa-yfc.org

Free Family Drop-ins and Lunch Bunches Monday through Friday.

Mequon Moms Club
www.mequonmomsclub.com

Mequon Moms Club offers playgroups, park dates and more!

Parents Place
570 E. Moreland Blvd.
Waukesha, WI 53186
(262) 549-5575
http://ppacinc.org/parent.php

Free Playgroups during the week for families with young children.

Do you have something to add? Email us at
miltownmoms@gmail.com.

CHAPTER 20: SCIENCE & TECHNOLOGY

If you have a little scientist on your hands, have fun exploring the places on our list to foster their curiosity and creativity. You can learn about the planets, be inspired at Discovery World's innovative exhibits, or roam the aisles at local science stores.

American Science and Surplus

6901 W. Oklahoma Ave.
Milwaukee, WI 53219
(414) 541-7777
http://www.sciplus.com

Stroll the aisles in American Science & Surplus and you're sure to find something wacky and inexpensive! This store offers science kits, educational toys, school supplies, arts and crafts items, hobby tools, scales, lab glass, housewares, electronics and more! They also offer family fun nights throughout the year.

Discovery World

500 N. Harbor Dr.
Milwaukee, WI 53202
(414) 765-9966
http://www.discoveryworld.org

Discovery World is the perfect place for young curious minds to explore. Besides their exciting exhibits, they offer workshops like "Food of the Future" that give kids access to hands-on, super-fun learning!

Engineering for Kids

(414) 247-1248
https://engineeringforkids.com

Engineering For Kids brings science, technology, engineering, and math (STEM), to kids ages 4 to 14 in a fun and challenging way through classes, camps, clubs, and parties.

UWM Manfred Olson Planetarium

1900 E. Kenwood Blvd.
Milwaukee, WI 53211
(414) 229-4961
http://www4.uwm.edu/planetarium/

The Manfred Olson Planetarium, located on the UWM campus, presents a variety of astronomy programs open to the general public. They also offer planetarium shows, activities & birthday celebrations. The Friday Night Show is just $2 with a special topic that changes every 4-6 weeks. AstroBreak on Wednesdays and Stargazing is free.

Retzer Nature Center Planetarium

Retzer Nature Center
S14 W28167 Madison St.
Waukesha, WI 53188
(262) 896-8007
http://www.waukeshaschools.com/planet/

The 40 ft. dome shaped ceiling in the Charles Horwitz Planetarium can recreate the day or night sky by projecting images of the stars, planets, the sun, and the moon. The Spitz 512 star projector can be set to show the sky for any date, time, or latitude. You'll be able to see 2,500 stars fill the sky like never before, complete with digital video and sound, special effects and interactive science displays. The planetarium offers year-round public programs, children's shows and family events.

Do you have something to add? Email us at
miltownmoms@gmail.com.

CHAPTER 21: SPECIAL NEEDS RESOURCES

If you have a child with special needs, one of the places or organizations in our resource guide might help to enrich your lives and navigate the challenges you may be facing.

ORGANIZATIONS

Easter Seals Southeast Wisconsin

2222 S. 114th St.
West Allis, WI 53227
(414) 449-4444
http://www.easterseals.com/wi-se

Easter Seals Southeast Wisconsin provides services to ensure that all people with disabilities or special needs and their families have opportunities to live, learn, work and play in their communities.

Independence First

(414) 291-7520
http://www.independencefirst.org/home

Independence First inspires kids and adults with all types of disabilities to build skills for self-sufficiency.

Life Navigators

7203 W. Center St.
Wauwatosa, WI 53210
(414) 774-6255
http://www.lifenavigators.org

Life Navigators provides opportunities and services for their children with intellectual and developmental disabilities.

Milwaukee Center for Independence

2020 W. Wells Street
Milwaukee, WI 53233
(414) 937-2020
http://www.mcfi.net

MCFI offers services to help children with disabilities, profound medical issues and special needs reach their full potential.

Office for Persons with Disabilities
901 N. 9th St., Room 307-B
Milwaukee WI 53233
(414) 278-3932
http://county.milwaukee.gov/OPD

The OPD provides services that make County programs, services, and facilities accessible to people with disabilities.

United Cerebral Palsy of Southeast Wisconsin
6102 W. Layton Ave.
Greenfield, WI 53220
(414) 329-4500
http://www.ucpsew.org

United Cerebral Palsy of Southeastern Wisconsin seeks to advance the independence, productivity and rights of citizenship for persons with cerebral palsy and other disabilities and their families in Milwaukee, Waukesha, Ozaukee, Washington, Racine and Kenosha counties.

Vision Forward
Vision Forward Association
912 North Hawley Rd.
Milwaukee, WI 53213
(414) 615-0100

Vision Forward seeks to empower, educate and enhance the lives of individuals impacted by vision loss through all of life's transitions.

PLAYGROUNDS

Possibility Playground
Upper Lake Park
Port Washington, WI 53074
http://possibilityplayground.org

Possibility Playground is a new kind of playground; one where children of all abilities are able to play together. It was built with children of all types of physical abilities in mind, and has been used by thousands of children and parents to blend the line between learning, therapy and playtime.

SUMMER CAMPS

Easter Seals Summer Respite Camps
2222 S. 114th St.
West Allis, WI 53227
(414) 449-4444
http://camp.eastersealswisconsin.com

Easter Seals Southeast Wisconsin provides summer respite camp programs for children, teens and adults with or without disabilities.

First Stage Next Steps
325 W. Walnut St.
Milwaukee, WI 53212
(414) 267-2929
http://www.firststage.org/en/Our-Academy/Next-Steps/

First Stage creates a safe space for all students to be creative and be themselves without judgment or fear of failure. Next Steps classes are designed to help students with autism take their next steps as an artist and a person, allowing them the opportunity to learn social skills among their peers while participating in theatrical and musical activities.

Sensational Summer Day Camp
Milwaukee Center for Independence
Harry & Jeanette Weinberg Building
2020 W. Wells St.
Milwaukee, WI 53233
(414) 937-2020
http://www.mcfi.net/Childrens-Programs/Summer-Camp.htm

This indoor program combines social and therapeutic opportunities for children living with autism or sensory disorders.

Do you have something to add? Email us at
miltownmoms@gmail.com.

CHAPTER 22: SPORTS & RECREATION

From exploring the lakefront to practicing yoga as a family, Milwaukee offers a plethora of options for getting out and active with kids of all ages. Use this guide to explore your interests or to find a new activity to try together.

BASEBALL & SOFTBALL

Helman's Driving Range & Mini-Golf
N56W19901 Silver Spring Dr.
Menomonee Falls, WI 53051
(262) 252-4447
http://helmansdrivingrange.com

Seasonal outdoor center offering an 18-hole mini-golf course, driving range & batting cages.

Mike Hegan's Field of Dreams
16701 W. Cleveland Ave.
New Berlin, WI 53151
(262) 781-7526
http://hegans.net

Batting Cage, Arcade and Party Center.

Milwaukee Baseball Academy
4200 N. Holton St.
Suite 200
Milwaukee, WI 53212
(414) 828-4777
http://milwaukeebaseballacademy.com

Milwaukee Baseball Academy is an indoor training facility for baseball players from age 4 to 18 years old. The 9600 square feet includes four batting cages (15' x 70'), pitching mounds, a workout area for speed and agility and a weight room. There is even a parent waiting room with a viewing window to watch your child work out, relax, and even enjoy coffee, wifi, and TV.

Prairieville Park
2507 Plaza Ct.
Waukesha, WI 53186
(262) 784-4653
http://www.prairievillepark.com

Seasonal family entertainment center with an 18-hole mini-golf course, batting cages & bumper cars.

BIKING

Milwaukee Bike & Skate Rental
1500 N. Lincoln Memorial Dr.
Milwaukee, WI 53202
http://milwbikeskaterental.com

Rent surreys (family bikes), tandem bicycles, go-karts & more and ride along Milwaukee's lakefront!

Milwaukee by Bike:
http://city.milwaukee.gov/bike#.U9AZwFYYFBU

Here you will find most everything you need to know to help you get around Milwaukee by Bike.

Oak Leaf Trail
Milwaukee County's Paved Multi-Use Trail Network
http://county.milwaukee.gov/OakLeafTrail8289.htm

This trail features 118 miles of multiple loops through all the major parkways and parks in the system. Loops are composed of off-road paved trails, park drives, and municipal streets.

Unicycling
Tuesdays from 5:00-7:00 p.m. in Red Arrow Park
https://www.facebook.com/MSOEUniClub

Presented by MSOE Unicycle Club, enjoy free unicycle lessons at Red Arrow Park Ice Rink Tuesdays from 5-7p.m. No skills or gear needed!

BOWLING

Kids Bowl Free

Visit www.KidsBowlFree.com to register for free bowling passes to be used at JB's on 41, Brown Deer Lanes and Classic Lanes in Greenfield. It's part of a national initiative to get kids bowling and spending more time with their family.

American Serb Hall
5101 W. Oklahoma Avenue
Milwaukee, WI 53219
(414) 545-6030
http://www.americanserbhall.com

AMF Bowlero Lanes
11737 W. Burleigh
Wauwatosa, WI 53222
(414) 258-9000
http://www.amf.com/bowlerolaneswi

AMF Waukesha Lanes
901 Northview Rd.
Waukesha, WI 53188
(262) 544-9600
http://www.amf.com/waukeshalanes

Sunday Funday - $5 per person for 2 Hours of Bowling every Sunday.

AMF West Allis Lanes
10901 W. Lapham
West Allis, WI 53214
(414) 476-9100
http://www.amf.com/westallislanes

Sunday Funday - $5 per person for 2 Hours of Bowling every Sunday.

AMF West Lanes
7505 W. Oklahoma
Milwaukee, WI 53219

414) 321-5050
http://www.amf.com/westlaneswi

Bay View Bowl
2416 S. Kinnickinnic Ave.
Milwaukee, WI 53207
(414) 483-0950

Bluemound Bowl
12935 W. Blue Mound Rd.
Brookfield, WI 53005
(262) 786-6280
http://bluemoundbowl.com

Brown Deer Lanes
4715 W. Bradley Rd
Milwaukee, WI, 53223-3627
(414) 354-4730
http://www.browndeerlanes.com
*Kids Bowl Free Participant (see above)

Circle B Recreation
6261 Hwy. 60
Cedarburg, WI 53012
(262) 377-8090
http://www.circlebrecreation.com
*Kids Bowl Free participant (see above)

Classic Lanes Oak Creek
7501 S. Howell Ave.
Oak Creek, WI 53154
(414) 764-1120
http://www.classiclanes.biz

Classic Lanes Greenfield
5404 W. Layton Ave.
 Milwaukee, WI 53220
(414) 282-6400
http://classiclanesgreenfield.com
*Kids Bowl Free participant (see above)

Grafton Pub & Bowl

1305 Wisconsin Ave.
Grafton, WI 53024
(262) 377-1660
http://graftonpb.com

JB's on 41

4040 S. 27th St
Milwaukee, WI 53221
(414) 281-8200
http://jb-on-41.com
*Kids Bowl Free participant (see above)

Kreuger's Entertainment Center

N87 W16471 Appleton Ave.
Menomonee Falls, Wisconsin, 53051
(262) 251-2340
http://www.kruegersentcenter.com
*Kids Bowl Free participant (see above)

Sussex Bowl

N64 W24576 Main St.
Sussex, WI 53089
(262) 246-6808
http://sussexbowl.com
*Kids Bowl Free participant (see above)

Village Bowl

N86W18330 Main St.
Menomonee Falls, WI 53051
(262) 255-1580
http://www.villagebowl.com
*Kids Bowl Free participant (see above)

Do you have something to add? Email us at
miltownmoms@gmail.com.

GEOCACHING

VISIT Milwaukee GeoTour
http://www.visitmilwaukee.org/geocache

VISIT Milwaukee planted 15 geocaches in Milwaukee's most vibrant neighborhoods, taking treasure-hunters along the shores of Lake Michigan, into local parks and onto the streets of historic neighborhoods. Geocaching is the perfect weekend activity for the whole family, and it's easy to do! All ages will enjoy this high-tech scavenger hunt.

West Bend, WI: Geocaching Capital of the Midwest
http://visitwestbend.com

West Bend is located in the hills of the Kettle Moraine and offers four museums, including the new Museum of Wisconsin Art. Explore nature trails, parks, a historic downtown and a variety of community events. West Bend is known as the Geocaching Capital of the Midwest™ and is a favorite destination for treasure hunters from around the region.

Letterboxing (low-tech geocaching)

Letterboxing is a family-friendly pastime that combines treasure-hunting, navigational skills, and rubber stamping to explore new places all over the city, country and world. Check out www.letterboxing.org to learn more.

Do you have something to add? Email us at
miltownmoms@gmail.com.

GOLF & MINI-GOLF

Night Glow Golf

Milwaukee County Parks Golf Courses

http://milwaukeecountygolfcourses.com/golf/proto/milwaukeecountygolfcourses2/niteglow/niteglow.htm

Nite-Glow Golf is an after-dark golf game for all ages. Tees, flag sticks, and holes are illuminated and golf balls are glow-in-the-dark. Tee times start at 8:30 p.m.

The First Tee

11350 W. Theodore Trecker Way

West Allis, Wisconsin 53214

(414) 443-3570

http://www.thefirsttee.org/Club/Scripts/Home/home.asp

The First Tee's mission is to impact the lives of young people in Milwaukee County by providing learning facilities and educational programs that promote character development and life-enhancing values through the game of golf.

GYMNASTICS & TUMBLING

Infinite Gymnastics
8989 N. 55th St.
Brown Deer, WI
(414) 371-9520
http://www.infinitegymnastics.com

Gymnastics, tumbling & yoga classes for kids.

LaFleur's Gymnastics Academy
W189n10991 Klienmann Dr.
Germantown, WI 53022
http://www.lafleursgym.com

Gymnastics classes and open gyms for all ages.

Wildcard Gymnastics
3545 N. 127th St.
Brookfield, WI 53005
(262) 923-7418
http://www.wildcard-gymnastics.com

Do you have something to add? Email us at
miltownmoms@gmail.com.

ICE SKATING

Red Arrow Park
920 N. Water St.
Milwaukee, WI 53202
(414) 289-8791
http://county.milwaukee.gov/RedArrow11930.htm

Free skating (with skate rentals available at a small cost) is offered January - March at this downtown landmark. Remodeled in 1999, the ice rink can fit around 100 people at a time and is conveniently located right next to a Starbucks, so you can enjoy a hot chocolate!

Pettit National Ice Center
500 S. 84th St.
Milwaukee, WI 53214
(414) 266-0100
http://www.thepettit.com

The Pettit National Ice Center is an indoor ice skating facility in Milwaukee, Wisconsin, featuring two international-size ice rinks and a 400-meter speed skating oval

Do you have something to add? Email us at
miltownmoms@gmail.com.

ROCK CLIMBING

Adventure Rock
21250 Capitol Dr.
Pewaukee, WI 53072
(262) 790-6800
http://www.adventurerock.com

Indoor and outdoor rock-climbing opportunities for all ages and abilities.

Bounce Milwaukee
2801 S. 5th Ct.
Milwaukee, WI 53207
(414) 312-4357
http://www.bouncemilwaukee.com

With routes ranging from child-friendly to extremely challenging, Bounce Milwaukee's custom-designed rock climbing walls are paired with TruBlue autobelays for an experience as safe as it is confidence-boosting. No previous climbing experience is needed, and we have no minimum age requirements - just ask a host to help you get started.

Open Climb
Urban Ecology Center
Riverside Park
1500 E. Park Pl.
Milwaukee, WI 53211
(414) 964-8505
http://urbanecologycenter.org

Stop in after work or school and enjoy climbing their three story rock wall. All equipment is provided and trained belayers are on hand to assist.

Do you have something to add? Email us at
miltownmoms@gmail.com.

ROLLER SKATING

Skateland
Locations in Cedarburg, Butler and Waukesha
http://skate-land.com

Incredi-roll Skate and Laser Tag Family Fun Center
10928 W. Oklahoma Ave.
West Allis, WI 53227
http://incrediroll-sk8.com

SAILING

Milwaukee Community Sailing Center
1450 N. Lincoln Memorial Drive
Milwaukee, WI 53202
(414) 277-9094
http://www.sailingcenter.org

Students learn boat handling, sail theory, rules of the road and they learn and practice crew overboard-maneuvering skills along with capsize recovery skills. Scholarships are available.

Milwaukee Yacht Club
1700 N. Lincoln Memorial Drive
Milwaukee, WI 53202
(414) 271-4455
http://www.milwaukeeyc.com

Sailing lessons for children 8 & up!

S/V Denis Sullivan Day Sails
Discovery World
500 N. Harbor Dr.
Milwaukee, WI 53202
http://www.discoveryworld.org/exhibits/s-v-denis-sullivan/

Climb aboard the world's only three-masted recreation of a 19th century Great Lakes cargo schooner for a two hour sail. When you step aboard the S/V Denis Sullivan, you can become part of our crew or sit back, relax, and enjoy. You are invited to help set the sails and take a turn at the helm while you enjoy Milwaukee's rich maritime past on the beautiful waters of Lake Michigan. Public sails on the S/V Denis Sullivan are perfect for all ages.

Pewaukee Lake Sailing School
Pewaukee Yacht Club
N22W28204 Edgewater Dr.
Pewaukee, WI 53072
(262) 691-9927
http://plss.org

Sailing classes for age 5 & up!

WATER FUN

Splash!
10636 N. Commerce St.
Mequon, WI 53092
262-512-SWIM (7946)
http://www.splashmequon.com

'Tosa Pool at Hoyt Park
1800 N. Swan Blvd.
Wauwatosa, WI 53226
(414) 302-9160
http://friendsofhoytpark.org

Cool Waters Family Aquatic Park
2028 S. 124th St.
West Allis, WI 53227
(414) 257-8098
http://county.milwaukee.gov/CoolWaters9156.htm

Country Springs Water Park
2810 Golf Rd.
Pewaukee, WI 53072
(262) 547-0201
http://www.countryspringshotel.com

Milwaukee Kayak Company
http://milwaukeekayak.com

Juneau Park Paddleboats
http://juneauparkpaddleboats.com

Wiberg Aquatic Center
Wirth Park
2585 N. Pilgrim Rd.
Brookfield, WI 53005
(262) 787-3901
http://www.ci.brookfield.wi.us/index.aspx?NID=109

YOGA FOR KIDS

Haleybird Studios
9207 W. Center St.
Wauwatosa, WI 53222
(414) 502-0856

Haleybird Studios offers kids' and family yoga classes for all ages, as well as Summer workshops.

OmTown Yogis
http://omtownyogis.org

OmTown Yogis is a yoga community in Milwaukee that provides monthly yoga classes at the Art Museum and in Milwaukee parks. Once in a while, they provide kids' classes in addition to their regular classes.

Storytime Yoga
Betty Brinn Children's Museum
929 E. Wisconsin Ave.
Milwaukee, WI 53202
(414) 390-5437

Betty Brinn Children's Museum holds a storytime yoga a few times a month for young children. Check their calendar for dates and times.

Do you have something to add? Email us at
miltownmoms@gmail.com.

CHAPTER 23: STORY TIME
OUR THREE FAVORITE STORY TIMES

Local libraries offer many story time options for young children, but the story times listed in this section offer a little something extra for you and your little ones.

Storytime in the Gallery
Every Saturday at 10:30
Milwaukee Art Museum
http://mam.org/artgeneration/programs/weekend-family-programs/

Come hear a story that relates to a work of art in the galleries, and then make a drawing inspired by what you have seen and heard. Every Saturday at 10:30. Meet at admissions. Free with museum admission.

Preschool Story-time at Barnes & Noble
Every Wednesday at 10:00 a.m.
Barnes & Noble at Bayshore
(Children's Section)
http://store-locator.barnesandnoble.com/storelocator/stores.aspx?x=y&

Come hear a story that relates to a different theme each week. A small art project or activity that has to do with story will follow.

Story-time Yoga
Select Tuesdays at 10:30 a.m.
Betty Brinn Children's Museum
http://www.bbcmkids.org/visit/index.php

Get moving with kids' yoga and story-time, free with museum admission. Register at front desk.

Do you have something to add? Email us at miltownmoms@gmail.com.

CHAPTER 24: FREE SUMMER FUN

In Milwaukee, it's easy to have loads of fun in the Summer without breaking the bank. All of the activities in this chapter are completely free, and there are ideas for a wide range of ages and interests. Soak up Summer without spending a dime!

Airplane Spotting
1200 block of E. Layton Ave.

If your kids love airplanes, the Airport Observation Area is sure-fire hit. Onlookers flock to this parking lot on the 1200 block of E. Layton Ave. to get an up-close look and hear the roar of the massive jet planes as they come and go. Tune into 88.5 to hear aircraft communication. You can pick up some Culver's custard down the road, sit out on the car hood and make a night of it.

Animal Feedings
Urban Ecology Center (Riverside Park)

Every Saturday at 1:00 p.m., help the staff feed the turtles, frogs, and other reptiles at the Riverside and Menomonee Valley locations.

A.W.E. Truck Studio
http://awe-inc.org

Seeing A.W.E's colorful mobile art studio parked in your neighborhood is even better than the ice cream truck. These bright mini-vans are stocked with loads of art supplies and friendly artists who lead creative projects. The vans travel around Milwaukee throughout the entire summer, and it's completely free to participate! Kids can drop-in to paint, create prints, and build sculptures while learning about famous artists and basic principles of design.

Beach Day! (pg. 104)

Find a new beach to visit in this guide to Milwaukee County Beaches.

Beer Gardens

Don't let the word "beer" fool you! The Beer Gardens in Estabrook Park and Humdbolt Park are family-friendly and near the playground. Kids can enjoy craft soda and traditional beer garden food.

Day Trips (pg. 43)

Check out our guide for information about these free day trips:

Henry Vilas Zoo (Madison)
Bookworm Gardens (Sheboygan)
Possibililty Playground (Port Washington)

Cedarburg Historic District (Cedarburg)
Holy Hill (Hubertus)
& more!

Explore Nature
Havenwoods State Forest
http://dnr.wi.gov/topic/parks/name/havenwoods/

Havenwoods State Forest offers free programming all Summer long including guided family nature hikes, preschool storytimes, and Junior Ranger programs!

Family Flicks
http://county.milwaukee.gov/FamilyFlicks21477.htm

Milwaukee County Parks offer free family movie nights throughout the Summer.

Farmer's Markets (pg. 56)

Enjoy fresh food, artisans and live music! Some Farmer's Markets offer special kids' activities.

Free Admission Days

Some of Milwaukee's most popular attractions offer free days for county residents. You just have to know when they are:

Betty Brinn Children's Museum: Third Thursday of every month from 5:00 - 8:00 p.m.

The Domes: Free on Mondays from 9:00 a.m. - 12:00 p.m. with proof of county residency (excluding major holidays).

Harley-Davidson Museum: Children under 5 always free.

Milwaukee Art Museum: Free admission first Thursday of each month. (Children 12 and under always free.)

Milwaukee Public Museum: Free general admission on Thursdays.

Geocaching
http://www.visitmilwaukee.org/geocache

VISIT Milwaukee planted 15 geocaches in Milwaukee's most vibrant neighborhoods, taking treasure-hunters along the shores of Lake Michigan, into local parks and onto the streets of historic neighborhoods. Geocaching is the perfect weekend activity for the whole family, and it's easy to do! All ages can enjoy this high-tech scavenger hunt.

Kid's Club at Bayshore

Bayshore Town Center offers free activities on select days throughout the summer. Past activities have included a Bounce House Party, Kids Yoga, a School of Rock music program and free outdoor concerts! All of their events are listed on Bayshore's calendar and on MiltownMoms.com's Event Calendar.

Letterboxing
http://www.letterboxing.org/BoxStateRegion.php?state=wi

Letterboxing is an intriguing pastime combining navigational skills and rubber stamp artistry in a charming "treasure hunt" style outdoor quest. A wide variety of adventures can be found to suit all ages and experience levels.

Library Fun (pg. 82)

Local libraries offer extensive weekly programming for families including music, jugglers, magic shows, nature exhibits, storytimes and more, completely free to you. Check out our Library Guide to find programs near you!

Little Free Libraries
https://maps.google.com/maps/u/0/ms?msa=0&msid=201860500793147213935.0004ac6e854ff1e35e434&hl=en&ie=UTF8&t=m&ll=43.035521,-87.966843&spn=0.120454,0.219383&z=12&source=embed&dg=feature

Little Free Libraries have been popping up all over Milwaukee, and there are probably a few near you! The concept is simple - anyone can construct a box for books and install it anywhere they like. The signs say "Take a book. Leave a book," and that's just what you should do! It's kind of like a treasure hunt, and you're sure to find something the kids will love. Find a Little Free Library on Google Maps.

Marcus Center Kidz Days
http://www.marcuscenter.org/outreach/kids-families/

Every Tuesday, Wednesday & Thursday from the end of June through the middle of August, the Marcus Center offers live, interactive, performing arts programming completely free. Partners include First Stage Theater, Rick Allen Magic Show, Milwaukee Public Library, Betty Brinn Children's Museum, Trinity Irish Dancers, Milwaukee Ballet, Wehr Nature Center, and Lucky's African Drumming. All of their events are listed on the MiltownMoms.com's Event Calendar.

Summer Concert Series

http://www.miltownmoms.com/#!free-summer-concert-guide/cpf9

Every night of the week, Milwaukee offers free family-friendly concerts. The Wonderful Wednesdays series in Lake Park is specifically designed for kids. Check out our Free Summer Music Guide for more information.

Tiny Doors
Humboldt Park (Bay View)

Searching for the three tiny doors in Humboldt Park makes for a magical summer afternoon! The Tiny Door Project is a national trend that puts a little magic back in our lives. (Hint: You'll find the Tiny Doors at the bottom of large trees just south of the pond.)

Tours & Tastings (pg. 146)

The Humane Society, the Jelly Belly Factory, and more! Find out which Tours & Tastings are free for you and your family.

Water Ski Shows
Waukesha & Pewaukee

Head out to Pewaukee or Waukesha for the night to enjoy a free water ski show!

Badgerland Waterski Shows: Free Home Shows Every Wednesday Evening from Memorial Day to Labor Day in Frame Park on the Fox River in Waukesha, WI. Shows Start at 7:00 p.m.

Pewaukee Lake Ski Show – 6:45 on Thursdays @ Pewaukee Lakefront Park.

CHAPTER 25: THEATERS

There is nothing quite like sitting through the excitement of a live performance, except of course if you're the one on stage. Whether you're looking for a kid-friendly play or acting and improvisation classes, Milwaukee is home to world-class children's theater opportunities.

First Stage
(414) 267-2929
http://www.firststage.org

The Family Series at the Todd Wehr Theater presents up to six plays each season, geared towards children from ages 3 and up to ages 10 and up. The First Steps series at the Milwaukee Youth Arts Center presents plays suited for children ages 3 to 6. First Stage Young Company is an advanced actor training program for high school students that presents a full-scale productions each season.

Schauer Arts & Activities Center
147 N. Rural Street
Hartford, WI 53027
(262) 670-0560
http://www.schauercenter.org

Located approximately 40 minutes northwest of Milwaukee, in the heart of the Kettle Moraine, the Schauer Arts & Activities Center is a performing and visual arts complex located in downtown Hartford, next to the Wisconsin Automotive Museum. The Schauer Center presents family-friendly performances all season long!

Skylight Music Theater
Broadway Theatre Center
158 N. Broadway
Milwaukee, WI 53202
(414) 291-7811
http://www.skylightmusictheatre.org

Skylight Music Theatre owns and operates the Broadway Theatre Center which houses two unique theaters: the 358-seat Cabot Theatre, and the 99-seat Studio Theatre. The Broadway Theatre Center is home to three performing theatre companies, the Skylight Music Theatre, the Milwaukee Chamber Theatre & Renaissance Theaterworks.

Sunset Playhouse
800 Elm Grove Rd.
Elm Grove, WI 53122
(262) 782-4431
http://www.sunsetplayhouse.com

Bug in a Rug Children's Theatre is a great way for children, students, and their families to experience live theater while learning about kindness, determination and friendship from troupes of professional actors! It is an interactive experience for the whole family, targeted for children ages 3-8. It is a casual and fun introduction to the performing arts where laughter and audience participation are strongly encouraged. Each performance has a theme and educational points targeted for this age group. Everyone is invited to come dressed in pajamas, and bring along blankets, pillows and stuffed animals to snuggle in for a great time at all of our performances.

Wilson Center for the Arts
19805 W. Capitol Dr.
Brookfield, WI 53045
(262) 781-9470
http://www.wilson-center.com

The Wilson Center offers a variety of performances and events that the whole family can enjoy! The Tales by the Fire Series presents three one-hour performances for children of all ages. Join us for seasonal storytelling by the fireplace in the Grand Hall! Family Films presents feature films on the Big Screen in the Harris Theater, complete with concessions.

Do you have something to add? Email us at
miltownmoms@gmail.com.

CHAPTER 26: TOURS AND TASTINGS

(Sprecher Brewery tours are surprisingly family-friendly, and you can taste gourmet soda!)

Tours and tastings are a great way to break the monotony of typical weekend activities. You'll learn something new, support local companies and products, and have fun doing it. The tours and tastings in this chapter are all kid-friendly, so have fun exploring!

Buddy Squirrel Candy & Nut Tour
1801 E. Bolivar Ave.
St. Francis, WI 53235
(414) 483-4500
http://www.buddysquirrel.com

Now under one roof, you can see Quality Candy making award-winning chocolates and Buddy Squirrel creating fabulous nuts, snack mixes and gourmet popcorns. Tours are available Monday through Friday, and they last about 30-45 minutes. Your tour will include viewing of the entire production facility along with a visit to our Factory Store. Tours cost $3.00 per person and free samples are given to all who attend the tour.

Cheese Factory Tour at Clock Shadow Creamery
138 W. Bruce St.
Milwaukee, WI 53204
(414) 273-9711
http://www.clockshadowcreamery.com/index.php/our-story/tours/

Looking for an original educational experience? Why not learn about one of the most delicious products that Wisconsin has to offer? Visit this local cheese factory and learn about the history of cheese making, answer mysteries like: "Why are cheese curds squeaky?" and "Why is Cheddar cheese yellow?" and sample fresh cheeses.

Doors Open Milwaukee
Fall, 2015
http://doorsopenmilwaukee.org

Milwaukee features world-class events and attractions, but no single event highlights the environment that these attractions occur in and around. On the weekend of September 20th and 21st, the fourth annual Doors Open Milwaukee event will open the doors to over 100 wonderful buildings free-of-charge to the public –buildings that hold hidden treasures and special stories – from churches to office buildings, theaters to work sites, museums to hotels, clubs to universities; all sites of historic, architectural, cultural, or commercial interest. And remember — if it rains, most of our activities are indoors.

Doors Open Milwaukee will designate 24 sites of special interest to families with children during the event. Those under 18 can pick up a free passport featuring all 24 at any designated passport site and have them stamped at each one visited. (Passports will be available to adults for $1).

Firehouse Tours
North Shore Fire Department
http://nsfire.org

Contact your local fire department for a kid-friendly tour! You'll get to climb on the fire trucks, try on a fire coat and learn all about fire safety. You'll also get a fire hat and a coloring book!

Hispanic Heritage Self-Guided Tour
United Community Center
1028 S. 9th St.
Milwaukee, WI
(414) 384-3100
http://www.unitedcc.org/Self_Guided_UCC_Tour.pdf

Marvel and learn about the colorful mural that pay homage to Hispanic heritage. End your tour in the Gallery at the Latino Arts Center.

Jelly Belly Factory
10100 Jelly Belly Ln.
Pleasant Prairie, WI 53158
(866) 868-7522
https://jellybelly.com/info/visit_jelly_belly/
wisconsin_warehouse

Sweet sensations and a world of delight await you at the Jelly Belly Visitor Center. Located in Pleasant Prairie, Wisconsin, near Kenosha and Racine, 30 minutes south of Milwaukee, and 90 minutes north of Chicago, the Jelly Belly Visitor Center features full-throttle fun on the FREE Jelly Belly Express Train Tour.

The Visitor Center is designed so visitors can take a tour of our warehouse (really, it's fun!) and taste the magic of the original gourmet Jelly Belly jelly bean. The 25-30 minute train ride makes stops at a variety of Stations with large screen video monitors showing the company's century of candy making and how we make candy corn, jelly beans, gummies and more.

From the start Mr. Jelly Belly flies overhead welcoming you to the tour. Once you hop on board the Jelly Belly Express Train you will see Jelly Belly Bean Art, a chorus line of dancing Jelly Belly characters, and giant Jelly Belly jelly beans overhead as you travel down "Candy Alley".

Miller Park
http://milwaukee.brewers.mlb.com/mil/ballpark/tours/index.jsp

Get a behind-the-scenes look at this impressive Milwaukee landmark.

Monuments & Statues Walking Tour
http://www.gpsmycity.com/tours/monuments-and-statues-tour-in-milwaukee-5691.html

Milwaukee is home to statues and monuments that entertain us, inspire us & honor our heroes. There are also very unusual statues such as a monument to a duck and its ducklings. Take this walking tour to explore Milwaukee's monuments and statues.

Sprecher Brewing Company
701 W. Glendale Ave.
Milwaukee, WI 53209
(414) 964-7837
http://www.sprecherbrewery.com/tours.php#ReserveTastings

On this kid-friendly tour, you'll visit the brew house and discover how Sprecher is reviving the Old World brewing traditions that once made Milwaukee famous. Travel through the lager cellar and see the Bavarian murals on display on the bottling room wall. After the brewery tour, the next best thing to Munich is Sprecher's indoor beer garden, with music and samples from any of up to 20 beers and 10 sodas on draught. Reservations required.

St. Joan of Arc Chapel
Marquette University Campus
http://www.marquette.edu/chapel/index.shtml

Could this be the oldest building in Milwaukee? Was it actually built in France? Come explore this fascinating building. Tours are free.

Trolley Loop
http://www.milwaukeedowntown.com/getting-around/
milwaukee-trolley-loop/

During the Summer, connect to downtown Milwaukee's festivals, museums, shops and events with the Milwaukee Trolley Loop. The 30-stop route links passengers to all the major attractions, and, best of all, rides are only $1 per trip. So whether you're an out-of-town guest or a tourist in your own town, hop aboard and get acquainted with all the things that make this city sizzle.

Wisconsin Humane Society
4500 W. Wisconsin Ave.
Milwaukee, WI 53208
(414) 264-6257
http://www.wihumane.org/about-us/shelter-tours

Take a behind the scenes tour of the Wisconsin Humane Society! Learn how shelter staff and volunteers help transform unwanted companion animals into much loved family members and how injured and orphaned wild animals get a second chance. Your guide will take you through the Wildlife Gallery, Veterinary Hospital, Guest Lodging and Adoption Avenue. Weekend tours are free and open to the public.

Do you have something to add? Email us at
miltownmoms@gmail.com.

CHAPTER 27: ZOOS & PETTINGS ZOOS

If your child is an animal lover, Milwaukee does not disappoint. From family-owned petting zoos to the impressive Milwaukee County Zoo, our city offer plenty of opportunities to interact with local animals or watch exotic animals from afar.

Bear Den Zoo & Petting Farm
6831 Big Bend Rd.
Waterford, WI 53185
(262) 895-6430
http://www.beardenzoo.com

The Bear Den Zoo and petting farm has been family owned and operated for over 25 years. What started as a simple love for animals, turned into a dream of conservation, preservation and education. The Bear Den Zoo has amazing exotic animals in addition to traditional farm and native wild life for you and your family to enjoy.

Concord Zoo
N6485 County Road F
Oconomowoc, WI 53066
(262) 593-5400
http://www.concordgeneralstore.com

Come pet and feed the animals at the Concord General Store Zoo in Oconomowoc. There are ponies, goats, pigs and more! There is no admission fee.

Green Meadows Petting Farm
33603 High Dr. (Hwy.20)
East Troy, WI 53120
(262) 534-2891
http://greenmeadowsfarmwi.com

Come meet all of our friendly animals at our educational animal farm petting zoo located in Waterford, WI. We offer both a hands-on guided or self-guided tour. Learn about our pigs, cows, goats, sheep, chickens, turkeys, ducks, geese, donkeys, horses and much more! Everyone can milk our friendly cow. We offer pony rides for children and a hayride to the "Back 40" of the farm. Play with the kittens in our "Kitty Barn." Relax in our picnic area with playground. Pick a FREE pumpkin from the Pumpkin Patch in Fall. Food, drinks and souvenirs available at the "Feedbag." The Farmers and Animals look forward to meeting you!

Milwaukee County Zoo
10001 W. Blue Mound Rd.
Milwaukee, WI 53226
(414) 771-3040
http://www.milwaukeezoo.org

As one of the country's finest zoological attractions, the Milwaukee County Zoo will educate, entertain and inspire you! Visit over 2,000 mammals, birds, fish, amphibians and reptiles in specialized habitats spanning 200 wooded acres. Explore educational wildlife shows, fun attractions and enticing special events.

Racine Zoo
2131 N. Main St.
Racine, WI 53402
(262) 636-9189
https://www.racinezoo.org

Shalom Wildlife Zoo
1901 Shalom Dr.
West Bend, WI 53090
(262) 338-1310
http://www.shalomwildlife.com

Wisconsin's Wildest Zoo offers the best in wildlife viewing! Journey along the three miles of trails and observe deer, elk, bison, wolves and much more in a natural environment. Explore the educational exhibits and markers along the way. Tour the Indian artifact museum, visit the children's play area & farm petting zoo or take a guided educational Wagon Tour!

Do you have something to add? Email us at
miltownmoms@gmail.com.

CHAPTER 28: JUST FOR MOM

No one said being a mom was easy. Fulfilling? Yes. Enjoyable? Mostly. But easy? No. With that in mind, we've put together lists and suggestions for you to make your life easier, enjoy a little down time every now and then, and connect with other moms.

FIVE APPS TO MAKE YOUR LIFE EASIER

Artkive
http://www.artkiveapp.com

What to do with all those art projects your kids bring home? Artkive them! This has saved me piles and piles of clutter. I just snap a picture of each art project my little guy brings home, and soon I can create a book of all his masterpieces! Best Part: I don't feel like a terrible mother when I (gently) place one of his scribbles in the garbage can.

MyHomework
https://myhomeworkapp.com

Does it seem like your kid is always on their phone? Why not download a MyHomework app so they can keep track of everything they need to do for school? It's colorcoded by due date so they'll know what to do first.

Cozi Family Planner
http://www.cozi.com

Finally. A mobile planner that everyone in the family can access and that's easy to use. Color coded by family member, this calendar will keep your whole family on the same page. Best Feature: Family Central with today's activities listed

Quizlet
http://quizlet.com

Here's another app to help your child study for any of their classes, particularly English and Foreign Language. As a teacher, I can vouch for this. It helps my students learn vocabulary at their own pace, and they honestly have fun doing it. Check it out if you're child could use some extra practice at home.

IFood Assistant by Kraft
http://www.kraftrecipes.com/media/ifood.aspx

Back to School - Back to Chaos. It's so hard to keep thinking of new, healthy, tasty dinners. But this app is the best one I've found for finding ideas and creating shopping lists. Best feature: You can enter what ingredients you already have, and it will pull up recipes that you can make with them.

DATE NIGHT & GIRLS NIGHT OUT

BREWERY TOURS

Great Lakes Distillery
616 W. Virginia St.
Milwaukee, WI 53204
(414) 431-8683
http://www.greatlakesdistillery.com

During the one hour tour, visitors will learn about the products, how and why we make them, and receive a flight of six products to try (complimentary soda is available for non-drinkers).

Historic Pabst Brewery
Best Place at the Historic Pabst Brewery
901 W. Juneau Ave.
Milwaukee, WI 53233
(414) 630-1609
http://bestplacemilwaukee.com

Relive the early years with a tour offering a free PBR, Schiltz, or a root beer. Enjoy retro beer commercials, step into the Captain's Courtyard, take a picture with Steamboat Captain Frederick Pabst, tour former Pabst Corporate Offices, including Captain Pabst's old office, the Board Room, Blue Ribbon Hall and much more. After the tour, hang out with your friends, soak up more of the Best Place atmosphere, and experience true German "Gemuetlichkeit!"

Lakefront Brewery
1872 N. Commerce St.
Milwaukee, WI 53212
(414) 372-8800
http://www.lakefrontbrewery.com/tour

Tour this industrious and inventive microbrewery on the Milwaukee River. The tours are high-energy and include a souvenir pint glass and four 6 oz. pours. Trip Advisor ranks this tour #4 in the country!

Miller Brewery
4251 W. State St.
Milwaukee, WI 53208
414-931-BEER (2337)
http://www.millercoors.com/AgeVerification.aspx

From your personal tour guide to the ghost of Frederick Miller, you will experience over 155 years of brewing history with a modern-day twist. International visitors and local guests alike experience something new with every tour. Commemorative photos, gift shop keepsakes and an unforgettable exploration of large-scale brewing await you! More importantly, you will end every tour with ice cold beer samples. Relax and enjoy your brew in a Bavarian-style Miller Inn or outdoor Beer Garden (seasonally) with friends and family at this historic Milwaukee landmark.

Milwaukee Brewing Company
613 S. 2nd St.
Milwaukee, WI 53204
(414) 226-2337
http://mkebrewing.com

Learn about local ingredients and suppliers in a sustainable, creative and innovative environment. The tour is "Beer in Hand" and samples are offered when you check in and for some time after the technical tour end.

Sprecher Brewery
701 W. Glendale Ave.
Milwaukee, WI 53209
(414) 964-7837
http://www.sprecherbrewery.com/index.php

Visit the brew house and discover how Sprecher is reviving the Old World brewing traditions that once made Milwaukee famous. Travel through the lager cellar and see the Bavarian murals on display on our bottling room wall. After the brewery tour, the next best thing to Munich is Sprecher's indoor beer garden, with music and samples from 20 beers and 10 sodas on draught.

Beer Gardens
http://www.miltownmoms.com/#!beer-gardens/c24oz

Find out about our area's family-friendly Beer Gardens.

COMEDY CLUBS

Comedy Cafe
615 E. Brady St.
Milwaukee, WI 53202
(414) 271-5653
http://milwaukeescomedycafe.com

Comedy Sportz
420 S. First St.
Milwaukee, WI 53202
(414) 272-8888
http://www.comedysportzmilwaukee.com/main_page.html

Jokerz Comedy Club
11400 W. Silver Spring Rd.
Milwaukee, WI 53225
(414) 463-5653
http://www.jokerzcomedyclub.com

Do you have something to add? Email us at
miltownmoms@gmail.com.

COOKING CLASSES & FOOD TOURS

Boelter SuperStore
4200 N. Port Washington Rd.
Milwaukee, WI 53212
(414) 967-4333
http://www.boeltersuperstore.com

Milwaukee Food & City Tours
(800) 979-3370
http://www.milwaukeefoodtours.com

Milwaukee Public Market
400 N. Water St.
Milwaukee, WI 53202
(414) 336-1111
http://www.milwaukeepublicmarket.org/classes.html

Superior Equipment & Supply
4550 S. Brust Ave.
Milwaukee, WI 53235
(800) 960-4300
https://www.superiorequipmentsupplies.com

Sur la table
Bayshore Town Center
480 W. Northshore Dr.
Milwaukee, WI 53217
(414) 332-2096
http://www.surlatable.com/category/Web-Cooking-Root/
Cooking-Classes?affsrcid=AFF0005

WINE & PAINT STUDIOS

A Stroke of Genius
250 W. Broadway
Waukesha, WI 53186
(262) 893-4186
http://www.paintwinestudio.com

Arte Wine & Painting Studio
Locations in Wauwatosa & Delafield
(414) 810-6095
http://artewineandpaint.com/!/

La Terraza
11520 W. Bluemound Road
Wauwatosa, WI 53226
(414) 443-1800
http://potteryfun.com

Splash Studio
184 N. Broadway
Milwaukee, WI 53202
(414) 882-7621
http://www.splashmilwaukee.com

Do you have something to add? Email us at
miltownmoms@gmail.com.

VINTAGE BOWLING ALLEYS

Landmark Lanes
2220 N. Farwell Ave.
Milwaukee, WI 53202
(414) 278-8770
http://www.landmarklanes.com

Koz's Mini Bowl
2078 S. 7th St.
Milwaukee, WI 53204
(414) 383-0560
http://www.kozsminibowl.com

American Serb Hall
5101 W. Oklahoma Ave.
Milwaukee, WI 53219
(414) 545-6030
http://www.americanserbhall.com

Do you have something to add? Email us at
miltownmoms@gmail.com.

MOM GROUPS

Extreme Moms
http://extrememoms.org

Extreme Moms organizes unique workshops and thrilling extreme sports events in and around Milwaukee just for mom.

Milwaukee Babywearers
http://www.milwaukeebabywearing.com/new/

Milwaukee Babywearers is a local, volunteer run group that promotes baby-wearing. They provide free classes, forums for discussions, and organized playgroups.

Mothering Arts Milwaukee
https://www.facebook.com/motheringartsmilwaukee

Mothering Arts connects and nurtures new mothers and their babies, and offers ongoing parent support. Join their summer Saturday series to form friendships with other moms. Babies will enjoy music and gentle touch. Each week a different wise woman from the community will share ways to nurture ourselves and better care for our families.

Mothering The Mother
http://motheringthemotherinc.info

Mothering the Mother is a non-profit dedicated to improving pregnancy, childbirth, and motherhood experiences for all women. They provide a lending library, prenatal care coordination services (PNCC), educational classes, birth doulas for continuous labor support, lactation support for improved breastfeeding success, postpartum doulas to help with the new transitions the family is experiencing, support groups, and mentors (sliding scale available to those who qualify).

We Run This
http://werunthis.org

We Run This is a women's running community in Milwaukee, online and in person.

PREGNANT IN MILWAUKEE

BIRTH CENTERS

Authentic Birth Center
530 N. 108th Pl.
Wauwatosa, WI 53226
(414) 231-9640

Centrally located in Wauwatosa, WI, just minutes from numerous area hospitals. Over 2000 square feet of multi-use space available for community classes, meetings and events from birth art to zumba.

Columbia Center
13125 N. Port Washington Rd.
Mequon, WI 53097
(262) 243-7408

Columbia Center is a specialty hospital dedicated exclusively to birth. It offers a modern, spa-like environment, which conceals the latest medical technology. They offer a doula program.

Well Rounded Maternity Center & Boutique
2455 S. Howell Ave.
Milwaukee, WI 53207
(414) 744-7001

Milwaukee and Southeastern Wisconsin's free-standing birthing center since 2004. The birth center offers waterbirth in a home-like, peaceful environment where freedom of movement in labor is encouraged. Midwives provide healthy prenatal care and support natural, un-medicated birth at the center or home.

Well-Rounded Maternity Center is also home to Bellies & Babies Boutique, which features a large selection of cloth diapers, baby carriers and resale maternity clothing.

The Center offers many classes and events.

Well-Rounded Maternity Center was named "Best Place to Have a Baby" by Milwaukee Magazine, 2011.

BREASTFEEDING STATIONS

If you prefer to nurse in private, here are locations designed specifically for nursing moms:

Betty Brinn Children's Museum: Nursing nook in the baby area in Pocket Park.

Buy Buy Baby (Brookfield): Nursing and changing station to the left of the entrance.

Bayshore Town Center: Nursing room near the restrooms off of the food court.

PRENATAL YOGA & FITNESS

Destination Maternity
16010 W. Blue Mound Rd.
Brookfield, WI 53005
(262) 786-9872

Destination Maternity offers FREE prenatal and postnatal classes in their in-store studio. Classes include Baby Yoga, Couples Yoga, Mommy and Me Yoga, Prenatal Pilates & Yoga, Pumping Pilates & Yoga, and more!

Haleybird Studios
9207 W. Center St.
Wauwatosa, WI 53222
(414) 502-0856

Haleybird Studios offers prenatal yoga classes twice a week in the evening, as well as specialty workshops and classes.

Invivo
2060 N. Humboldt Ave.
Milwaukee, WI 53212
(414) 265-5606

Invivo offers Prenatal Yoga classes and Mom & Baby Yoga Workshops. They are located in the Riverwest neighborhood of Milwaukee in a serene, modern studio overlooking the river.

CHAPTER 29: BEST OF THE BLOG

Kids and technology: what's OK?
Nov. 1, 2013

It starts early, this epic battle with technology that we parents face. It's a love-hate relationship, really. We love technology for the times that it distracts our children so that we can cook dinner. We love it for the times that it teaches them new things, or helps them to complete their homework. We love it for the times that it helps them channel their imagination and create something new.

But for all of the good things technology brings our kids, we fear the dangers, too. Cyberbullying, sexting, child predators, obscenities, childhood obesity, and gaming addictions are just a few of the risks we take when we enter this ever-growing technological labyrinth.

The overprotective mom in me wants to keep my kids sheltered from these dangers. But deep down I know that that would be like building a fence around a pool. I can keep them out for awhile, but what I really need to do is teach them to swim.

In order to fully understand the dangers of technology and how dependent we have become upon it, naturally I turned to technology. I Googled and Googled and Googled. I wanted to learn how to help my children navigate their world in a healthy, moderate way. I tried to separate the good advice from the bad advice from the completely unrealistic advice. And I found some patterns in my research.

Here is a guide to the best advice I found:

1. **Know the facts:** According to one of most comprehensive surveys done by the Kaiser Family Foundation, kids are spending over seven hours a day in front of a screen for enjoyment, or almost a third of each day. But what is more surprising from this survey is that over two thirds of respondents indicated that they had no rules or limits for the amount of screen time they were allowed. While technology can benefit kids in many ways, unsupervised, unrestricted screen time can expose them to images and behaviors you wouldn't dream of having them exposed to otherwise.

2. **Start young**: If possible, start guiding your children and setting limits while they're still young and you're still their favorite person. This will give you

credibility from early on, and solidify you as the source they can rely on when questions arise.

3. **Teach "Netiquette:"** Just as you teach them to say "please" and "thank you," teach them about technology etiquette from a young age. This may include not allowing texting during meals or not typing in all caps, for example. As they mature, talk regularly about building an appropriate online reputation and identity, just as you would hope to build in "real life." Remind them that the same rules for kindness and respect apply online, so if they wouldn't say something in real life, they shouldn't type it either. Finally, talk openly about the permanence of online behavior and about the possible consequences of irresponsible actions.

4. **Set limits:** No one said parenting was easy, but it's our job to establish values, limits and insist on accountability. The American Academy of Pediatrics recommends no more than two hours a day of screen time for kids over two. (Before two, they recommend none. But come on.) They also recommend that you allow no screen time during meals or after bedtime.
In addition to these time limits, experts recommend keeping computers and other gadgets outside of the bedroom in a central place. A central location makes it easier to monitor what your kids are doing online. Some experts suggest that you insist on being your child's friend on Facebook and follow them on whatever social networks they're plugged into.

"Psychology Today" recommends establishing from the beginning that you know your child's passwords and can review their online activity regularly. Finally, your kids should see technology as a privilege that can be restricted or revoked if established rules are not followed. In other words, if grades slip, or attitudes get ugly, the X-box may need to live in the attic for awhile.

5. **Be the change:** Monkey see, monkey do. Just as modeling healthy eating habits is the best way to get our kids eating right, modeling the technology use we want to see is the most effective way to shape our kids' behaviors. It may be easier said than done, but it certainly is important. Catherine Steiner-Adair, a clinical psychologist at Harvard Univeresity, has interviewed countless families about this topic.

Sadly, one thing she heard over and over again from kids is how sad and angry they feel when they have to compete with a cell phone or tablet for their parent's attention. The bottom line is that kids notice when you're on your phone at every stoplight, at dinner, or during bath time. According to Steiner-Adair, not only can these behaviors strain our relationships with our kids, it can also reinforce the behaviors we don't want to see.

6. **Use your resources**: Educate yourself with free parent guides to popular social networks at <u>connectsafely.org</u>. Consider using Net Nanny or a similar program to keep your internet connections free of all the nasty stuff, and be sure all of your security settings are on highest for social networks.

7. **Have unplugged fun**: Some families have started weekly traditions of having a designated "Unplugged Night" where they spend time together and no technology is allowed. You can enjoy a favorite meal, play some good old-fashioned board games or head to the park. No doubt moments will arrive when you all want to reach for you phone, perhaps just to settle an argument with a quick Google search. But if you make the challenge of being "unplugged" into more of a game, it can be a special bonding time for your family.

8. **Take your technology outside:** Geocaching is a great way to incorporate technology and GPS devices into an active lifestyle. If you have kids who love using technology, this high-tech treasure hunt may be the perfect way to get them moving and exploring the world while keeping them connected to their favorite device.

Raising grateful kids
Nov. 25, 2013

Thanksgiving is right around the corner, and many of us are counting our blessings and pausing to appreciate what's really important in life. But are we raising our kids to be thankful, as well?

Studies have shown that grateful kids are not only happier kids, but are also more likely to have higher grades, more friends and more life satisfaction than their materialistic counterparts.

They're also less likely to abuse drugs and alcohol, have behavior problems at school or suffer from depression.

So it's no wonder parents are wondering how to make their kids more thankful.

According to the experts, encouraging "please" and "thank you" is a great place to start, but true gratitude – and the empathy and compassion that comes with it – is a long-term process and requires real effort on the part of parents.

An ounce of prevention

Although it's difficult to say no in a culture that celebrates consumerism and all things new and shiny, that's exactly what's necessary. It's hard to teach thankfulness to kids if they get everything they ask for.

So if you're serious about raising grateful kids you'll have to say no even when it seems easier – and maybe more fun – to say yes.

One clever psychologist suggests having "look days" and "buy days."

Before you head out for the day's activities, let your kids know that it's just a "look day." Maybe you'll see trees at the park, or toys in the store or souvenirs at the museum, but today you're just looking and enjoying. Other days can be "buy days," when you purchase things. Of course, more days should be "look days" than "buy days."

Think of saying "no" to new materials things as saying "yes" to appreciating what you already have.

To avoid an unreasonable amount of gifts and materials things at holiday time, consider Secret Santa exchanges where everyone receives one or two special items. If you can't avoid the deluge of gifts, be sure to keep the focus on celebrating and spending time with friends and family rather than the gifts.

And of course, help your child write thank-you notes for each gift they receive. Young children might start out just drawing a picture and scribbling their name. As they get older, it's nice to explain why the like the gift and what they'll do with it.

Rituals

If you don't already, it might be nice to incorporate some kind of thankfulness ritual into everyday life. At dinnertime, for example, you might start out the meal with everyone mentioning one thing they're grateful for from that day. Some families say grace or a prayer before their meal to give thanks for the food they're about to eat.

Bedtime is another great time for kids to reflect on what they're thankful for. Whatever it is, dedicating one time per day to building gratitude goes a long way to raising a grateful child who is aware of their blessings.

Work for it

To fully appreciate the work that gets done around the house, kids need to participate regularly and consistently in the household chores. They're more likely to be truly grateful for the things that are done for them if they've experienced the kind of work that goes into it.

Another great way to foster empathy and compassion in your children is to involve them in service projects in the community. No matter your child's age, there are projects big and small that can help them connect to others in a meaningful way and be more grateful for the things they have. For some ideas, see our guide to Family-Friendly Community Service.

Model it

As with anything else, we parents have to be living examples of what it means to be grateful. Thank your child when they deserve it. Talk about what you're grateful for. Live your life in a way that prioritizes people over things.

And when you master this wonderful, idyllic list I've put forth for us all, please let me know how you did it!

Family-friendly Milwaukee Bucket List - 2014
January 2, 2014

I'm seven months pregnant. I have a two and a half year old who goes to bed at 7:30. Let's face it - my New Year's Eve won't exactly be glamorous. (Although I may allow myself one whole Diet Coke, just to get really crazy.) However, I am looking forward to a year of beautiful memories with my growing family. Here is my attempt at creating the quintessential Milwaukee Bucket List for Families for 2014.

1. Ice skate at Slice of Ice in Red Arrow Park, and warm up with hot cocoa afterwards!

2. Rev up a motorcycle (within the safe confines of the Experience Galley) in the Harley Davidson Museum.

3. Find all 15 geocaches planted in different Milwaukee neighborhoods by VISIT Milwaukee.

4. Feed the animals and reptiles at the Urban Ecology Center in Riverside Park or the Menomonee Valley on any Saturday or Sunday.

5. Play with the worms at Growing Power (Public Tours are held Sundays and Mondays at 1 p.m.)

6. See a bald eagle up close at Word with a Bird at Schlitz Audubon Nature Center, every Saturday and Sunday at 1-2 p.m.

7. See the 85-foot Kapok tree in the Tropical Dome at the Mitchell Park Domes, free to county residents every Monday morning from 9-12.

8. Tour the Milwaukee Art Museum with a free, self-guided Art Pack made for kids, free all day long every first Thursday of the month.

9. Check out a family drop-in at COA in Riverwest.

10. Find one new letterbox a month (Don't know what letter boxing is? You should! Check it out here.

11. See a First Stage show.

12. Go to storytime in the Gallery at the Art Museum, held every Saturday morning.
13. Go "grocery shopping" in the child-size Sendik's store at the Betty Brinn Children's Museum, free on the third Thursday night of every month.

14. Explore the exhibits by flashlight at night at the Milwaukee Public Museum for a museum overnight. There's a different theme each month!

15. Hear the Festival City Symphony at a Pajama Jamboree at the Marcus Center or Symphony Sunday at the Pabst Theater.

16. Check out all the Free Music nights in the summer.

17. Visit each Milwaukee County Beach at least once.

18. Go galactic bowling at JBs on 41 on Saturdays & Sundays at 6 p.m.

19. Enjoy the view of Lake Michigan while eating an ice cream cone at North Point Custard.

20. Pet a fish in the aquarium at Discovery World.

21. Slide down the Triple Dog Dare water slide at Country Springs Water Park.

22. Fly a kite at a Gift of Wings Kite Festival in Veteran's Park.

23. Make a snowman and go sledding in Humboldt Park in Bay View.

24. Camp in the Kettle Moraine State Forest.

25. Attend a "Tuesdays in the Garden" event at Lynden Sculpture Garden in Brown Deer.

26. Go on a Butterfly Quest at Havenwoods State Forest.

27. Churn butter, walk on wooden stilts & meet the blacksmith at Old World Wisconsin.

28. Run around Possibility Park in Port Washington.

29. Slide down Bernie's Slide before a Brewer's Game.

30. Visit the Saxe Brothers Movie Palace in the Chudnow Museum of Yesteryear.

31. Ride the Safari Train at the Milwaukee County Zoo. Family Free Days happen once a month in January, February, March, April, November, & December.

32. Bike along the Oak Leaf Trail.

33. Enjoy free kids programming at Milwaukee Central Library every Saturday for Saturdays at Central.

34. See the model aircrafts at the Mitchell Gallery of Flight at the airport.

35. Do a community service project as a family.

36. Try falafel, schnitzel, and burek at the Holiday Folk Fair.

37. Give myself a break from cooking and eat at a family-friendly restaurant.

38. Tour the Jelly Belly Warehouse Factory (and eat some jelly bellies, of course!)

39. Attend each one of the festivals at Henry Maier Festival Grounds.

40. Tumble around at LeFleur's Gymnastics Academy in Germantown.

41. Rollerskate at one of Skateland's locations in Butler, Cedarburg or Waukesha.

42. Spend a day in the country at Green Meadows Petting Farm in East Troy.

43. Have a picnic at Hawthorn Glen, explore over 23 acres of woodland and prairie, then visit their hands-on nature center.

44. Compost with Kompost Kids at their demonstration and education events, held every Saturday from 12 to 2:30 p.m.

45. Go apple picking.

46. Eat fresh food and explore local artists at area farmers' markets.

47. See Milwaukee from afar from the Holy Hill Observation Tower.

48. Take a family yoga class at Haleybird Studio in 'Tosa.

49. Paint your own pottery at Art Trooper in Fox Point.

50. Ring in the New Year the family-friendly way: at noon! The Betty Brinn Children's Museum hosts a New Year's at Noon party each year on Dec. 31.

3 guidelines for talking to a pregnant woman

January 15, 2014

OK, people. I get it. There is something about the sight of a pregnant woman's belly that causes us to smile inside, hold open the door and strike up a friendly conversation. I love to chat with people about how far along I am, if the nursery is complete and if we've thought about names. (OK, I don't love the last one, but I can deal with it.)

However, like many other pregnant women, I don't enjoy listening to all of the unsolicited comments about my changing and growing body. In the presence of a pregnant belly, it's as if all social norms become obsolete.

Throughout my last two pregnancies, I have received many well-intentioned comments about my body, both positive and negative.

"Wow, you're really showing now."
"You don't even look pregnant!"
"All of the sudden, you look really pregnant."
"From behind I can't even tell."
"It must be time to deliver soon!"
"You must be really uncomfortable."
"You look tired."
"Are you pregnant?"

Much like when a woman is not pregnant, there are some simple rules of etiquette to follow when it comes to sharing your thoughts on her body.

Here are three simple steps to follow when deciding whether of not to comment on a pregnant woman's body. Read on if you don't want to be the jerk who offends or annoys an innocent expectant mother:

1. First, ask yourself if you are a man. If you are a man, don't comment on the pregnant woman's body.

2. Next, ask yourself if you are a good friend of the pregnant woman. If you are not, don't comment on the pregnant woman's body.

3. If you are a woman, and you are a good friend of the pregnant woman, you may proceed with commenting on the pregnant woman's body. Here are some appropriate comments to choose from:

"You look amazing."

"You're glowing."
"You look so healthy."
"You're gorgeous."
"You are the most beautiful pregnant woman I've ever seen in my whole life."

Get the idea?

If any other thoughts or judgments enter your mind that aren't wildly positive and supportive, and you are considering saying them out loud, return to step No. 1.

5 steps to getting your kids to tell the truth
July 7, 2014

I've always been afraid of the moment that my pure and innocent young child would knowingly lie to me for the first time. I imagined that I would feel terribly sad to realize that he wasn't a perfect and divine being, but rather human, just like me.

Surely it would be awhile before I would have to deal with this fall from grace. I wondered what his first lie would be about. Would he lie about getting in trouble at school? Eating unhealthy foods? Not doing his homework?

So it surprised me when I found crayon all over the dining room table, and my three year old responded in broken, staccato English "I not know you're talking about, mama!"

My sweet young boy. Those big blue eyes. Lying through his tiny teeth.

Luckily, a recent study out of the University of Toronto gives us some helpful hints for how to teach our children of all ages to tell the truth:

1.) Relax. The experts assure us that lying is a normal part of development, and due in part to children's wild imaginations.

2.) Focus on the positive. Rather than give moral explanations for why lying is bad, focus on the positive benefits of telling the truth. Children in the study lied less after hearing the George Washington cherry tree story than when they heard "Pinnochio" or "The Boy Who Cried Wolf." In all of the studies, kids responded better to hearing the virtues of a protagonist who heroically told the truth about chopping down his father's favorite cherry tree, rather than stories that focused on why lying is bad.

3.) Help kids develop empathy. According to the experts, we can encourage good moral behavior by focusing on the effects our behavior has on others. Talk with your child about how their lying might affect their family and friends. This advice extends to other behavior, as well. For example, instead of scolding your child for hitting another child, focus on the child who has been hit. Ask if they're okay and tend to their wounds before talking with your child about their poor decision.

(I've tried this to reinforce positive behaviors, as well. If my child is sharing, I ask him to notice how happy he has just made the other child. I'll get back to you on if this works or not.)

4.) Ask kids to "promise." For whatever reason, these researchers found that kids were much less likely to lie if they had been asked to say "I promise." So there ya go.

5.) Model honesty. There it is again: The experts telling us that we need to model the behavior we wish to see in our children. However, in addition to telling the truth ourselves, they also stress we must be honest about what our expectations are. If we tell our children that we will not get mad at their transgression as long as they tell the truth, then we better control our temper when they admit to spilling juice all over the laptop.

Five back-to-school tips from teachers
August 27, 2014

Back-to-school time can mean excitement and stress for the whole family. To lighten up the latter, I asked teachers from around the country to dish out some back-to-school advice for parents. Their answers were sometimes serious, sometimes funny, and always served with a dash of insight only teachers can offer.

1. Be caring, but not overbearing.

Overwhelmingly, teachers stressed the importance of keeping a delicate balance between being involved with your child's education, while also affording them freedom to grow.

Teachers encouraged parents to keep in touch via email, read the syllabi sent home in the beginning of the year, and familiarize themselves with online grading systems. Parents should try their best to stay on top of daily assignments and activities.

But teachers stressed that it's equally important to allow your children to make mistakes and learn from the consequences that are given to them.

As one high school history teacher put it, "Support them in their efforts to be successful, but allow them to feel the sting of disappointment when they fail to execute. Failure feels bad! Success feels good!"

2. Be positive.

Maybe math was not your favorite subject. Maybe you can't speak a lick of Spanish after four solid years of high school classes. Who says that will be your child's experience with the subject?

Many educators I spoke with encouraged parents to stay positive with children about their classes, even if they had a negative experience themselves with the subject. One foreign language teacher says, "It's okay to share struggles but too often I think students think their parents' trouble areas in school are genetic and feel defeated before they even start. Let your child form his or her own experiences and be positive as much as possible!"

3. Praise the struggle, not the smarts

If you see your child struggling, try to view it as a good thing, rather than an uncomfortable state that you want to prevent. One teacher advises, "Let the student struggle sometimes. It is good for them to go through a little adversity."

As parents and teachers, it makes sense to encourage a "growth mindset" from a young age, which emphasizes the value of struggle and challenge to the education process. On the other hand, simply complimenting a child on how intelligent they are, without any emphasis on the necessary effort and work, might lead students to avoid failure at all costs in order to maintain their sense of being smart.

4. Sleep

Back-to-school time can easily become a whirlwind of long to-do lists, extra-curricular activities, and staying up late doing homework. But the teachers I spoke with emphasized the importance of balance and rest. One teacher said with a smile, "Sometimes this means saying to a child, 'Put down Harry Potter, it's time to turn off the light.'"

5. Want the Wi-Fi Password? Not so fast.

When all else fails, use your leverage as a parent to help your child stay focused. One particularly clever teacher advises, "Change your WiFi password daily/weekly. In this new age of social media, it's an immediate incentive point for parents to leverage!"

CHAPTER 30: EXCLUSIVE OFFERS

Cut out the exclusive offers in this section to save at family-friendly establishments around town. Enjoy!

Present this coupon for
ONE FREE
MUSEUM ADMISSION
when purchasing one admission
at the regular price.

betty brinn
children's museum
929 E. Wisconsin Ave., Milwaukee • 414-390-KIDS (5437)
www.bbcmkids.org

Limit one per person/family. Not valid with any other offer. Expires 12/31/15.

FAMILY GUEST PASS

SCHLITZ
Audubon
NATURE CENTER

1111 E. Brown Deer Rd. • Milwaukee WI • 53217
www.SANC.org • 414.352.2880
Open 9:00am - 5:00pm • 7 Days a Week
(Check for extended Summer Hours)

Schlitz Audubon offers six miles of trails that take
visitors through 185 acres of forests, wetlands,
restored prairies, ravines, bluffs, and a shoreline
beach, along with enviromental education programs
for all ages.

EMAIL: _____

EXP. 12/31/16 - NOT VALID FOR SPECIAL EVENTS

Families LOVE JB's on 41!

Receive a $5 game card with any bowling purchase

BOWLING, GAMES, FOOD & FUN!

4040 S. 27th St.
Milwaukee, WI 53221
414-281-8200
facebook.com/jbson41

Expires on December 31, 2015

No cash value. Not valid with any other coupons or specials. One coupon per group per visit. Offer valid for one $5 game card per group.

MBLOG14

FAST·FIRE'D

BLAZE 🔥 PIZZA

FREE PIZZA

WITH THE PURCHASE OF REGULARLY PRICED PIZZA
17530 WEST BLUEMOUND ROAD
BROOKFIELD. WI 53045

www.blazepizza.com 262-754-0999
Must present coupon. No copies allowed.
Expires 12/31/15 Cashier Code: 120

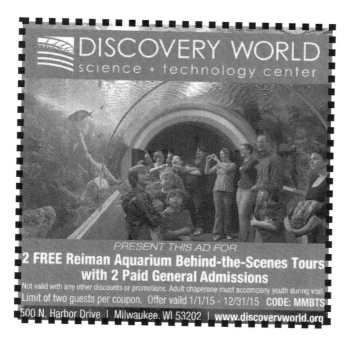

37816224R00122

Made in the USA
Lexington, KY
14 December 2014